RELIGION IN PUBLIC LIFE

Also by Dan Cohn-Sherbok

THE JEWS OF CANTERBURY
ON EARTH AS IT IS IN HEAVEN: Jews, Christians and Liberation Theology
THE JEWISH HERITAGE
HOLOCAUST THEOLOGY
JEWISH PETITIONARY PRAYER: A Theological Exploration
RABBINIC PERSPECTIVES ON THE NEW TESTAMENT
THE CRUCIFIED JEW: Twenty Centuries of Christian Anti-Semitism
ISSUES IN CONTEMPORARY JUDAISM
THE BLACKWELL DICTIONARY OF JUDAICA
DICTIONARY OF JUDAISM AND CHRISTIANITY
EXPLORING REALITY (*editor*)
THE SALMAN RUSHDIE CONTROVERSY IN INTERRELIGIOUS
   PERSPECTIVE (*editor*)
THE CANTERBURY PAPERS: Religion and Modern Society (*editor*)
ISLAM IN A WORLD OF DIVERSE FAITHS (*editor*)
TRADITION AND UNITY: Sermons Published in Honour of Robert Runcie
   (*editor*)
A TRADITIONAL QUEST: Essays in Honour of Louis Jacobs (*editor*)
THE SAYINGS OF MOSES (*editor*)
USING THE BIBLE TODAY: Contemporary Interpretations of Scripture
   (*editor*)
WORLD RELIGIONS AND HUMAN LIBERATION (*editor*)
PROBLEMS OF CONTEMPORARY JEWISH THEOLOGY (*editor*)

Also by David McLellan

ENGELS
KARL MARX: Early Texts
KARL MARX: His Life and Thought
KARL MARX: Selected Writings
KARL MARX: The Legacy
MARX
KARL MARX: Interviews and Recollections (*editor*)
MARX: The First 100 Years
IDEOLOGY
MARXISM AND RELIGION
MARXISM AFTER MARX
MARX BEFORE MARXISM
MARX'S *GRUNDRISSE*
THE THOUGHT OF KARL MARX
THE YOUNG HEGELIANS AND KARL MARX
SIMONE WEIL: Utopian Pessimist
SOCIALISM AND MORALITY (*editor with Sean Sayers*)
SOCIALISM AND DEMOCRACY (*editor with Sean Sayers*)

Religion in Public Life

Edited by

Dan Cohn-Sherbok
Lecturer in Jewish Theology
University of Kent at Canterbury

and

David McLellan
Professor of Political Theory
University of Kent at Canterbury

St. Martin's Press

Selection and editorial matter © Dan Cohn-Sherbok and David McLellan 1992
Introduction © Christopher Lewis 1992

Chapter 1 © Keith Ward 1992	Chapter 6 © Julia Neuberger 1992
Chapter 2 © Edward Norman 1992	Chapter 7 © Chris Rowland 1992
Chapter 3 © Tony Benn 1992	Chapter 8 © Enoch Powell 1992
Chapter 4 © John J. Vincent 1992	Chapter 9 © Digby C. Anderson 1992
Chapter 5 © Hugh Montefiore 1992	Chapter 10 © David McLellan 1992

First published in Great Britain 1992 by
THE MACMILLAN PRESS LTD
Houndmills, Basingstoke, Hampshire RG21 2XS
and London
Companies and representatives
throughout the world

A catalogue record for this book is available from the British Library.

ISBN 0–333–53557–X hardcover
ISBN 0–333–53558–8 paperback

Printed in Hong Kong

First published in the United States of America 1992 by
Scholarly and Reference Division,
ST. MARTIN'S PRESS, INC.,
175 Fifth Avenue,
New York, N.Y. 10010

ISBN 0–312–07279–1

Library of Congress Cataloging-in-Publication Data
Religion in public life / edited by Dan Cohn-Sherbok and David
    McLellan.
        p.   cm.
    "The following is a series of lectures given in Canterbury
    Cathedral Library in late 1990 and early 1991"—Pref.
    ISBN 0–312–07279–1
    1. Religion and politics.   2. Religion and state.   I. Cohn
-Sherbok, Dan.   II. McLellan, David.
BL65.P7R436   1992
261.7—dc20   91–32830
                                                      CIP

Contents

Preface   vii

Notes on the Contributors   ix

Introduction: Religion in Public Life   1
   Christopher Lewis

1   Is a Christian State a Contradiction?   5
   Keith Ward

2   Christian Politics in a Society of Plural Values   17
   Edward Norman

3   Religion, War and the Gulf   29
   Tony Benn

4   Christian Discipleship and Politics   38
   John J. Vincent

5   Religion and the Politics of the Environment   51
   Hugh Montefiore

6   The Prophetic Tradition and Human Rights   64
   Julia Neuberger

7   Liberation Theology and Politics   74
   Chris Rowland

8   Reading the Gospels Seriously   91
   Enoch Powell

9   How Can We Discharge our Obligations to the Poor?   98
   Digby C. Anderson

10 Unto Caesar: The Political Relevance of Christianity   110
   David McLellan

Further Reading   122

Index   124

Preface

The following is a series of lectures given in Canterbury Cathedral Library in late 1990 and early 1991. We would like to thank the Cathedral for offering us its hospitality, and particularly Canon Christopher Lewis and Mrs Charlotte Hodgson. The cost of the lectures was supported by the Board of Studies in Politics and International Relations at the University of Kent, the Centre for the Study of Religion and Society, and the Cathedral itself. Finally, we would like to thank the citizens of Canterbury and the students of the University for their lively contributions to the discussions following the lectures.

DAN COHN-SHERBOK
DAVID MCLELLAN

Notes on the Contributors

Dr Digby Anderson is director of an independent social policy 'think-tank', The Social Affairs Unit. A sociologist, he is the author of numerous books, scholarly articles and newspaper columns in *The Times*, *The Sunday Times* and *Sunday Telegraph*.

The Rt Hon. Tony Benn was first elected to the House of Commons in 1950, serving as a Cabinet member for eleven years, and on Labour's National Executive Committee. He is the author of twelve books including four volumes of political dialogue.

Rabbi Dr Dan Cohn-Sherbok is University Lecturer in Jewish Theology at the University of Kent.

The Rev. Canon Dr Christopher Lewis is a Canon Residentary of Canterbury Cathedral.

Prof. David McLellan is Professor of Political Theory at the University of Kent and author of the recently published *Simone Weil: Utopian Pessimist*.

The Rt Rev. Hugh Montefiore was formerly Dean of Caius College, Cambridge, and later Bishop of Birmingham and acting Chairman, Friends of the Earth Trust.

Rabbi Julia Neuberger is a visiting fellow at the King's Fund Institute, shortly to take up a Harkness Fellowship at Harvard University for six months. She is concerned with issues of health, race, citizenship and ethics, and is a trustee of the Runnymede Trust and of the Citizenship Foundation.

Dr Edward Norman is Chaplain of Christ Church College, Canterbury, formerly an historian, who has written on aspects of Church and State relations in modern times.

The Rt Hon. Enoch Powell was Fellow of Trinity College, Cambridge from 1934 to 1938, and Professor of Greek at the University of Sydney from 1938 to 1939.

The Rev. Professor Chris Rowland teaches New Testament at Oxford University and chairs the Latin America and Caribbean Committee of Christian Aid.

The Rev. Dr John J. Vincent has been Director of the Urban Theology Unit and Superintendent of the Sheffield Inner City Ecumenical Mission since 1970, and was President of the Methodist Conference, 1989–90.

The Rev. Professor Keith Ward is Regius Professor of Divinity in the University of Oxford. He is Chairman of the World Congress of Faiths and a member of the Council of the Royal Institute of Philosophy.

Introduction – Religion in Public Life

Christopher Lewis

Perhaps religion is the same as politics: it is political activity under cover of God. Or are they entirely separate pursuits, religion being an individual and spiritual matter whereas politics is for the collective and material world? A characteristic answer from Christians is that religion is to do with the whole of life and involves all kinds of ethical choices, although (and here an 'of course' often slips in) it is not party-political. So religion, it is said, is inevitably political for it provides a critical perspective on public life. Then we might move on to ask whether politics are inescapably religious; is political decision-making ultimately lost without the backing of a religious world-view in the light of which the politics make sense?

The debate is endlessly intriguing. The same person who says that Churches should keep out of political life in Britian may have been found supporting the activities of the Church as a focus for dissent in Poland. Perhaps that is reasonable, for the countries have very different histories and are markedly dissimilar in their social and religious structures. Yet if what is true in one contemporary context is false in another, how do we interpret the significance of the Old Testament prophets in their social context or of Jesus in his? It is to them that many would go for a way forward. So the debate is not only intriguing; it is also deeply serious for it concerns the relationship of two of the most fundamental human activities.

In such a debate, simple answers are elusive, but there are approaches which are illuminating and helpful to the seeker after truth. We decided to tackle the subject by collecting a talented and varied group of people to lecture and discuss in the cathedral reading room. The intention was to throw light on different facets of religion as it plays a part in public life. It is appropriate to do that through the partnership of two neighbours: a cathedral and a university, linked through the Centre for the Study of Religion and Society. Not that one of these bodies represents 'religion' and another 'public life', but rather that the subjects intertwine in the life of all institutions. Canterbury Cathedral is at times accused of failing to bring a religious or moral critique to bear on its own dealings with the world. The University of Kent, a secular foundation, often has opportunities

1

to reflect on its relationship to religion. Should it, for example, have an explicitly religious building on the campus, and if so where and for whom? We are never only examining others; we are also scrutinizing ourselves.

If public life and religion should enjoy a close relationship then they ought perhaps to be linked institutionally at the highest level. Keith Ward focuses on England as he reflects on what it might mean for there to be a Christian state. He is against a 'magisterial' conception of establishment where the Church is expected to lay down the law for the people. Rather, in the context of a robust defence of liberalism, he supports a 'ministerial' or deliberately weak version of establishment, where the Church – in this case mainly the Church of England – is the prime resource for shaping the values and beliefs both of the individual and of the community. Even if a 'stronger' view of establishment were possible in a pluralistic society, it would be undesirable for it would deny basic Christian principles concerning the freedom of the individual. In response to questions, Keith Ward presented a light version of the post-Reformation rule *'cuius regio, eius religio'* (each person's religion depends on the country in which he or she lives), for every country needs a coherent moral and religious resource.

The relationship of Church to State is the subject of Edward Norman's paper also, but his approach is very different. For he sees no possibility (or desirability) of a 'Christendom' model in a modern pluralist society where different moral and spiritual agencies compete, the Churches among them. He welcomes the virtual abandonment of the use of religious justifications for the actions of the State and says that the Church should not seek power. The Church should pursue its spiritual task which concerns the sin and salvation of individuals; the state should allow it to do so without interference.

From studies of the relationship between State and Church, we move to the question of what action follows on from faith: what should we do and not do? Tony Benn spoke on the day when the Gulf War cease-fire was declared and that gave a powerful context for his reflections on war. He holds the view that religious belief leads to strong moral and political stances, for example the duty to save life and the duty to understand the history and hidden interests in a particular situation. War depends on the de-humanizing of the enemy and leads to the concealing of moral issues. It must therefore be opposed.

In his paper Tony Benn moves quickly between moral principle and political interpretation. John Vincent also seeks to act politically, but works with a more explicit theology. He sees the Gospels as identifying Christians as radical disciples. It is no good being a cultural 'insider' and trying gently to influence society as so many do; the Christian story has to be rediscovered in practice in urban and liberation terms. For John Vincent, Christianity is transparently political, stemming from Jesus' own teaching and activity.

In John Vincent's terms, Hugh Montefiore's paper is for 'insiders' as well as 'outsiders'. A particular ethical challenge is addressed: the ecological crisis facing the planet. Here is a wealth of material in support of the case that both churches and governments should do more. The role of the Church is to assert first principles and clarify morality, while bringing pressure to bear on government so that we may be better stewards of the environment.

A further argument for pressure to reform comes from the liberal Jewish position. Julia Neuberger finds in the prophetic tradition firm ground on which to establish duties and rights: the call to justice and equity springing from the command of God. She sees the principles as universal and therefore refers not only to the Jews, but also to London's homeless and to the plight of the Palestinians.

Prophetic biblical material is thus used and guidance discovered for the contemporary world. That relationship between Bible and world is also a prime concern of the next two papers. Christopher Rowland's study of liberation theology gives an account of the Latin American experience where basic communities meet to reflect first on their lives and then on the Bible – context then text. God in the Bible is seen as one who identifies with those who suffer injustice and the communities meet, committed to social change.

For Enoch Powell, however, the text is a matter of fascination as an object for study. He finds the sweeping conclusions often drawn from the Bible inappropriate, for the text must first be studied with great care. In the discussion after his paper he was asked whether his own political views had been influenced by his reading of the Bible and he replied that the influence was only of the most indirect kind.

The theme of reticence is continued by Digby Anderson who charts the complex picture which he finds before those seeking to engage in welfare work today. The obligation to help is unchanging but the means is not. He attacks the Churches for simplistic and sloppy thinking in their attempts to enter complex areas and to solve problems. State welfare is in crisis and he recommends helping the neighbours who live immediately around us.

Within what framework do we reflect on these diverse contributions to the debate over the place of religion in public life? David McLellan attempts to provide such a framework in the final contribution, while at the same time stating his own view that the religious perspective on political problems is crucially important. Is religion irrelevant to politics; is it just a means for giving political arrangements legitimacy; is it first and foremost a critical perspective on policy; is it . . . ? I hope you find the questions and indeed the answers as helpful as did those who heard the lectures delivered.

1 Is a Christian State a Contradiction?
Keith Ward

Is a Christian State a contradiction? It may seem strange to raise this question at Canterbury, the home of the primate of a Christian state. For despite much vociferous talk of England being a multi-cultural, multi-faith society, in fact it is a Christian country, in which the monarch is bound to defend the Christian faith established as the religion of this country by law. Of course what is meant by establishment is rather unclear. I suspect most people think it means that the government controls and financially supports the Church of England. No doubt the government often wishes it did control the Church, and the Church wishes the government did pay the clergy or pay for the maintenance of its buildings, as it does in many communist states; but neither of these things is true.

The Queen is the supreme governor of the Church (not its head, a title which Henry VIII took for a time). Formally, the monarch appoints bishops, and Parliament decides the forms of service and many matters of organisation. But in practice this is a rubber-stamping operation, and when Parliament rejected revision of the Prayer Book the Church simply ignored it. The Church has bishops in the House of Lords and tends to have access to government ministers on important issues. But its part in political decision-making is tiny, and confined to providing advice, along with many other bodies, including, increasingly, other major religious bodies. The Christian religion is taught in schools, but usually in conjunction with some other religions; and the form of Christianity taught is largely non-denominational; it is thus a very diluted form of established religion.

When people were fined for non-churchgoing; when all professions were closed to all but Anglicans; then one could say Christianity in its Anglican form was the official religion of England. But even then, nonconformity was a powerful influence in the country; and now Roman Catholics are as politically active as Anglicans. The establishment, it seems, is a mere relic of a failed attempt to make all true Englishmen into Anglican Protestant Christians. At a time when even half the Anglicans would deny they are Protestant, the anachronism is clear. When only ten per cent of the population go to Anglican churches, is this a Christian country now?

5

The real question is, should it be a Christian country? And what would be meant by that? What would a Christian country be? It would presumably be a country which upheld Christian beliefs, practices and values. All or at least the great majority of its members would profess the creeds, attend the public rituals and live by Christian moral principles, which would presumably be sanctioned by law. But what happens to dissenters? Perhaps they would be imprisoned, or tolerated as groups deprived of many privileges of state membership. Even John Locke, in one of the first important defences of toleration in English history, held that atheists and Roman Catholics should not hold public office, since they could not be trusted.

Should Christian beliefs, rituals and values be enforced by law? Should any beliefs about human nature and destiny be enforced by law? In Britain, and not only in Communist Russia or Muslim Saudi-Arabia, they have been: when the Act of Assent was in force, as a necessary condition of holding public office. But in Britain such assent was connected with the defence of the monarchy; assent to the articles of the Church of England was a declaration of loyalty to the Crown, in the days when Catholics were called upon by the Pope to overthrow the monarch and Puritans opposed the monarchy as such. The very existence of the Church of England was a political act of secession from foreign religious influences on British policy, though it enabled the Reformation to sanctify this political break with Rome and give it the martyr's seal of approval.

There is no doubt that medieval Catholicism often made claims to political supremacy. Pope Boniface claimed the right to appoint monarchs; and matters of international order were for long considered well within the Church's domain. But in England the break with Rome rejected such Catholic claims, placed the Church under the control and protection of the monarch in Parliament, and thus brought about the collapse of a unified European Christian authority. It also opened the way to the eventual destruction of the very idea of a Christian state.

There are a number of arguments for the view that Christian beliefs, practices and values should be sanctioned by penal law; that assent to them should be required for holding public office, and that the public expression of competing beliefs should be prohibited. This could be called the 'strong view' of a state or established religion. One argument is that if God is believed to have revealed the truth, then unbelief is a rejection of God and must be due to hardness of heart or wilful blindness. Christian beliefs and values may be thought to be so obviously correct that one cannot even understand disbelief. A second argument is that people are easily corrupted and easily led by peer-group pressure. Thus one cannot permit the promulgation of immoral (non-Christian) teachings, as that will lead to a lack of moral vision, to moral disunity, uncertainty and confusion. Thirdly, unbelief may lead to the loss of eternal life, and if one can prevent that possibility by censorship of beliefs, one should do so. Fourthly, if people claim the right to believe whatever they want, error and superstition will become rife and the divine teaching authority of the Church will be undermined.

All these arguments can be culled from the writings of various Roman Catholic theologians prior to the dramatic declaration of religious liberty at Vatican 2 – a declaration which Pope John Paul I confessed he found hard to accept. Why, after all, should grievous error have any rights? However, it was the Protestant Reformation which in effect undermined all these arguments. Firstly, it required that a clear distinction be made between what God reveals and what the Church says God has revealed, or how it is interpreted. Since the Reformers rejected much of Catholic teaching, they had to hold that the rejection of the beliefs of any institution or person is not necessarily synonymous with the rejection of God. The Reformation licences the possibility of sincere dissent from religious authority. Though Protestants did not always pursue the point to its logical conclusion, this entails that the right of conscientious dissent, and therefore of freedom of belief, is established. Once that happens, one can no longer justify the attempt to impose beliefs by law.

Secondly, if most people really are rather stupid and weak, and if those in authority are somehow exempt – perhaps by Divine help – from this general malaise, then one might grant to a wise and benevolent authority which possesses the truth social control in all matters of faith and morals. But if the authority is believed to be neither wise nor benevolent, if it is in fact believed to be doctrinally and morally corrupt, this control will quickly be revoked. A strong belief in the universality of sin, to which religious institutions are particularly prone (did not the religious establishment arrange for the death of Jesus?), will prevent one from handing over moral authority of this sort to any church or state. Protestant criticism of the Catholic Church as corrupt thus undermines the idea that one institution should be morally authoritative for the whole of society.

There must naturally be laws on morally sensitive and disputed topics – laws on divorce, abortion and euthanasia, for example. But though laws permitting or prohibiting specific practices must be promulgated, they need not be so on the authority of some church body. Such laws can be enacted through a due process of legislation, by a legislature which is replaceable or democratically revisable, and which can reflect general opinion in the country. In this process, religious bodies are free, together with others, to express their beliefs, seek to persuade others by fair means, and endeavour to change the law. There need be no morally authoritative body which can enact such laws unilaterally for the people. Protestant belief in the corruptibility of institutions and the almost irresistible temptations of power strongly suggests that it is wiser to institute a series of democratic checks on the power of such self-appointed authorities. A claim to teaching authority for the faithful can be allowed, but not a claim to legislative authority for the whole population.

Thirdly, the unbelief which leads to the loss of eternal life cannot be prevented by any external law. Protestants held that faith is a matter of the heart which cannot be imposed by law. If anything, the imposition of professions of faith by law will only lead to hypocrisy and thus compound sin, not prevent it. This view led to an emphasis on the indiscernibility of the motives of the heart, and a general distrust of any attempt to enforce conformity of belief by law.

Fourthly, for Protestants faith was said to be a matter of decision, of choice, not of reception by infant baptism into the Church. So personal freedom of decision came to assume great importance. Of course that freedom ought to be exercised to choose to trust God; but the price of such freedom is that sin will also become inevitable; all the more room, it will be said, for grace to abound. Autonomy, the freedom of the will to choose for or against God, becomes a primary value for Protestantism, and the mere repetition of credal formulae only ensures supine conformity, not purity of heart.

In all these ways the Reformation placed a new emphasis on the right of dissent from religious authority; on the corruption, and therefore the criticizability of all institutions; on the ineffectiveness of legal constraints in matters of faith; and on the value of autonomy, as the right to choose one's beliefs. There may be problems lurking in these values that the Reformers did not pursue. But they succeeded, historically, in laying the foundations for the liberal secular state. Such a state is the child of the splintering of religious authority at the Reformation. For once that was done, the claim of freedom of belief must outweigh any attempt to enforce any set of religious beliefs by law. The liberal State, as one in which freedom of the individual is highly prized, and the secular State, as one in which no religious belief is enforced by law, already came into existence at the Reformation as an idea, if it did not become a reality for some time.

It should not be thought, of course, that the Catholic Church had been entirely innocent of these ideas. Christianity abandoned the idea of a divinely revealed law for society in its earliest days, when it abandoned

Torah. In its place, the Catholic Church developed an ethical system based on the central doctrines of God's creation of a good universe and the creation of human beings in the image of God – an image given concrete form in the person of Jesus. Humans, sharing to some extent in Divine rationality, were said to be capable of working out the basic moral laws by reflection on the divinely created structures of nature. Natural Law became the basis of Catholic moral teaching. Insofar as the natural law lays universal duties upon all human beings, it reciprocally grants rights to all human beings. For what I have a duty not to do to anyone, you have a right to expect that I shall not do to you. Thus the fundamental principle of respect for persons is founded on their universal human rights, as children of God. That principle, when more fully thought out, implies respect for the conscientious and carefully considered beliefs of others. That, in turn, implies the freedom of all to follow conscience in matters of belief – a principle upon which the Catholic Church has always insisted. Again there are paradoxes lurking not far below the surface of this principle; but recent Catholic teaching has made it quite clear that this is a fundamental principle of Christian belief. As such, it probably always should have outweighed the paternalism which sought to enforce religion upon whole societies. But it took the Reformation to bring that point to the fore.

In sum, it seems, perhaps surprisingly, that the idea of a liberal secular society is in fact implicit in both Catholic and reformed theology. The surprise is due to the fact that faith is often opposed to liberal secularism as a radically different philosophy. The liberal, it is sometimes said, believes nothing in particular, and actually takes pleasure in seeing lots of different beliefs co-exist. She will only condemn what harms other people, where harm is whatever the victim considers to be harm. She regards variety of belief as an aesthetically pleasing phenomenon. The person of faith, however, must be wholly committed to the object of her devotion. She is bound to regret diversity of belief and try to bring all others to know the truth. She will think that people may well be mistaken about what will harm them, and will believe that any deviation from the true purpose of creation is to be lamented. The secularist will ignore or oppose religion and treat it as irrelevant to social and moral life, whereas the person of faith must believe that God's will for social and individual life is of paramount importance. Reference should be made to it in all important matters. What could be more different, then, than liberal secularism and religious faith?

This picture, however, is overdrawn. It is true that once the Enlightenment was freed of its religious origins it embarked on a strangely ironic

course. It began by calling for the overthrow of blind obedience to tyr-
annical and obscurantist religious authorities and recommending sub-
mission to the dictates of pure reason alone. But as it pursued the
implications of the death of God and the scientific picture of human
beings as having arisen because of blunders in the copying mechanisms
of DNA, reason, too, began to lose its authority. It came to be seen as
merely irrelevant scum on the surface of the central nervous system, a
mechanism with some survival value but no true objectivity. Thus starkly
seen, reason gave way to the will to power and the dominance of
desire as the only final authority in human life. It is at that stage
that the most extreme forms of liberalism simply say, 'Do as you please',
and may find an aesthetic pleasure in the variety of beliefs, since none
of them are objectively true or finally significant. It is at that stage, too,
that extreme secularism finds religion to be no more than a sad superstition, with no serious claim to truth to make.

These extremes in which Western culture to some degree finds itself
are due precisely to the separation of liberal secularism from religion.
The antidote is not the overturning of secularism, but its proper recon-
nection with faith. Religious forms of liberalism do not say that anything
goes. On the contrary, the claim of theistic liberalism is a strong and
committed moral claim that roots human freedom in the freedom of God.
Its permission of dissent is grounded in the virtue of tolerance, which is a
respect for, and an attempt to understand properly, the beliefs of others. It
in no way condones evil or indifference; but it expresses a belief in
the intrinsic worth of human nature, because of its creation by God.
Secularism, too, need not connote hostility or indifference towards religion. A secular society accepts that the diversity of faiths requires a fairness in their treatment and a common respect if it is not to degenerate
into hatred and misunderstanding.

It is clear to anyone who studies world religions that equally informed,
intelligent, sincere and holy people have quite different religious beliefs.
They cannot all be true; they ultimately appeal to incompatible authorities,
all claiming truth. Rarely do any of them convince adherents of the
other traditions. It is odd to impose one system by force on the ground
that it is true (even though one may believe it is true), when that truth
is widely disputed by the best authorities. In any case one should not
compel others to say that they believe something when they do not. So
one must permit the expression of dissent. Respect for the beliefs of
others requires that one must not impose ritual practices which express
one's own beliefs on others, or prohibit their practices, as long as they
do not conflict with the deeply held moral principles of the community.

All this suggests that the strong view of establishment is not compatible with Christian teaching and that the basic Christian values of tolerance, respect and fairness make such a strong view of a Christian state unjustifiable. Of course, although in England the Church is established by law, few, if any, could argue for the strong view of establishment. Whereas one might once have made the profession of the 39 Articles a test of loyalty to the English Crown, it is no longer necessary, or even plausible, to do so. That is perhaps just as well, since the 39 Articles have never commanded the assent of all English people, and perhaps few Anglicans could assent to them just as they stand. The convolutions Anglican ordinands go through to avoid assenting to them in any obvious way is a testimony both to the ambiguity and to the obsolescence of the articles. But if one gives up that standard of faith, it is hard to know just what form of Christian faith would be enforced. Critical study of the Bible, a greater sense of the ways in which history and culture influence the interpretation of beliefs and the acceptance of the basic world-view of the natural sciences have put many traditional formulations of religious beliefs in question. The Church of England is now itself, and perhaps always has been to some extent, a pluralistic institution, one in which diverse interpretations even of quite basic beliefs have been permitted. So there are real questions about which Christian beliefs are to be insisted upon. The strong view of the Christian state is not only unjustifiable; there are fundamental disagreements between Christians about what it could possibly be.

But there is another possible view of establishment, which we might call the 'weak view'. A particular religion could be sanctioned in society, by the maintenance of institutions (like universities or schools) for encouraging religious understanding and practice. One would not be compelled to hold specific beliefs (dissent would still be permitted). But certain intellectual disciplines and spiritual practices might be positively supported by the state as an important contribution to the life of the community. They might be thought of, for example, as supportive of moral effort and vision and as capable of providing incentives to seek social welfare and justice. As Robert Bellah put it in *The Broken Covenant*, 'Any coherent and viable society rests on a common set of moral understandings about good and bad . . . these common moral understandings must also in turn rest upon a common set of religious understandings that provide a picture of the universe in terms of which the moral understandings make sense'. A sense of the importance of religious belief and practice might lead to the desire to encourage both the personal search for meaning and value which is religion's main concern and the provision of a communal tradition within which such a concern can be met. This would be so only as long as the society (in our case, represented by the monarch in Parliament) did so approve of and desire these beliefs to be encouraged. But if, and insofar, as it is desired to encourage the understanding and practice of religion, one might reflect that one cannot simply support religion in general (some religions might be morally or intellectually dubious). One should therefore support a religion that is open and tolerant of others, that provides a ritual context that is symbolically rich and morally effective, a set of beliefs that allows for a diversity of interpretation and a set of values that can be widely shared and appreciated.

In any society we will, either explicitly or implicitly, be taught a view of history, of art, morality and of the world, which seeks to cultivate in us certain values, a sense of things worth doing. We are trained in a number of intellectual skills; and virtues are excellences in the realisation of such skills. Insofar as skills are taught, virtues are taught. One gets an idea of what things are worth doing and excelling at. These form basic values for the rest of our lives. If this is so, education is necessarily a training in virtue, in the virtue of learning, of knowledge and understanding, of truth.

The virtues of 'secular education' are those of the disinterested pursuit of truth, the use of the experimental method and the criticism of all authorities. Why is this secular? Because it does not seek to inculcate any belief about God or about an ultimate purpose in human life. In not doing that, of course, it may suggest that the pursuit of such a purpose is not of ultimate importance. If it were, if there were a skill in religious practice, and if it were considered to be of great importance, then it would be taught and valued. Its omission shows that it is not highly valued by society as such.

Or it may simply be that there is too much disagreement about such ultimate purposes; so there is no agreement about what religious skills are. What is the point of being very good at praying, if there is no God? In a secular state, religion is either regarded as unimportant or it is admitted that attitudes to it are too deeply divided to permit of any common practice. From the religious viewpoint, it cannot be a good thing that religion is treated as unimportant. But is it good that attitudes are deeply divided, that religious diversity exists? Extreme liberals would say it is. For people should be free to form their own beliefs, and the more different beliefs there are the better. Society will be richer, more variegated; more options will be open. Plurality and variety may be good in themselves, since they increase human choice – like having lots of theatres to choose between. One may hold that it is good to pursue questions of ultimate meaning and destiny freely and personally, and not be compelled to hold any one view. Yet it is still odd to think that it is a good thing that people disagree about such matters. Surely it cannot be good to disagree about ultimate truth?

But consider, as a comparison, the case of physics: it is not a good thing that scientists disagree about the nature of matter, for such disagreement shows that many of them lack the truth, which cannot be good. Yet it may be a good thing that science is such that disagreement is permitted; that creative options can be explored; and that truth may arise out of disagreement. One has to be very careful to distinguish the value of disagreement in itself, which is low, from the value of disagreement as a way of learning, which may be high. Dialectic, after all, was Plato's highest form of enquiry; and it requires disputation. Perhaps there is a value in free enquiry, in coming to learn certain things for oneself; in pursuing one's own understanding of the world. If so, disagreement will be an inevitable result of this good: without it, learning would not take place.

It is even possible that the raising of certain questions – about human destiny, the ultimate reason for existence and the meaning of one's own life – has an importance which does not lie in the possibility of providing any definite answers to them. Perhaps it leads to a reflective life, a life of self-examination and intellectual humility. Such questions may not have any answer: rather, they may express a realisation of the importance of certain attitudes towards life – attitudes of awe, non-attachment and liberation from triviality. There are certainly strong values asserted here; values of free enquiry, dispassionateness and liberation from undue attachment to disputed beliefs. In such a context, disagreement may seem a great good, as a means of seeing partialities, learning intellectual limits and discarding ill-stated opinions.

This is even more obvious in the case of the arts, where creative disagreement is the fuel of new invention and discovery. So discovery may be good; and disagreement may be its inevitable result. In that case, disagreement may be consequentially good. It partly depends upon whether one thinks religious truth is just obvious, a matter of accepting clear truths, or a matter of difficult discovery, requiring reflection and imaginative insight. One reason for taking the latter view is that religious belief just obviously is highly disputable. One response to this is to regret it and find it puzzling that others do not agree with one's own views. Any world-view which does not command universal assent needs to have some account of why others reject it. One common account is that everyone but oneself is blind or depraved, and thus cut off from the true light of truth. The trouble is, to an unbiased eye others seem just as intelligent, well-informed and morally sincere as oneself. So a more plausible course is to accept disagreement as a pointer to the nature of religious truth as something to be discovered only by a dialectical process of personal exploration. Then it will not be puzzling that others disagree; one will expect that. Indeed, a key religious virtue will be that of creative search together with a degree of agnosticism about matters of ultimate truth. There will still be a virtue to teach: the virtue of exploring questions of meaning and purpose sensitively and seriously. But one set of beliefs will not be represented as the obvious truth.

This is a view of religion as a personally appropriated understanding of the meaning and goal of life. It enshrines a clear belief that religion is a freely adopted commitment which permits plurality of beliefs. If it does not applaud plurality as such, it nevertheless applauds the fact that plurality is permitted, and accepts plurality as a consequence of what it does applaud – free enquiry into meaning and truth. One has here a sense of the importance of religious questions – questions about human nature and destiny, about ultimate values. And one places a high value on free enquiry and criticism as methods of seeking truth.

But it is not enough to explore religious questions intellectually, to be always critical and questioning. To appreciate moral and religious teaching, one needs to be inducted into a moral and religious community; one needs a knowledge of religious practice as well as knowledge of theory, even if one is free to reject it. In this respect, the Christian faith can be seen as a resource for personal transformation in relation to a supreme value. It will no longer claim an authority which all are obliged to accept. Nor will it claim to be the only spiritual resource. But it may be a good thing that a religious tradition which relates a community to its past spiritual resources and which is open and responsive to new currents of thought should be available to express and help to shape the basic values of the community.

The Church of England almost fits this picture. This is still seen by some as a weakness, but they see a religion as a club which should have hard and fast rules for its members. If it is a resource, then people can draw from the treasures of its tradition what they will and still be free to pursue truth in their own way. A Christian State, then, might be one which is concerned to provide spiritual resources for its people, especially at key moments in their lives, and which takes the Christian tradition in one of its forms as its main resource, without excluding others. It will be unsympathetic to any attempts to impose religious commitment on its people, by Acts of Assent or so forth. But it will not wish to ban all forms of spiritual symbolism and ritual from its public life. In our historical situation, it seems right that Christianity, as the main historical resource in Britain, should have a major part to play. But other forms of faith may be brought in, wherever possible, to complement this tradition. What we cannot return to is a state whose laws are exclusively Christian for all its members. What we can have is a state in which religion plays a positive role in giving vision, insight and inspiration to its people; and in which, therefore, an established Church might both play this role and encourage other denominations and faiths to play their part in it, too. But I confess that it is not as yet clear whether the Church of England is ready to play such a role. There are some indications that it is relapsing into a sort of sectarian purism, insisting that its members keep some fairly hard rules of belief and practice. This is in line with the retreat to fundamentalism being experienced by so many faiths throughout the world, wherein racist, nationalist and fideist boundaries are drawn which exclude and oppose all others. It is no accident that this goes along with calls to disestablishment, since it is clearly seen that with such a small proportion of the population being orthodox Christians, a purist Church can no longer seriously claim to speak for the people or minister to their spiritual needs. However, there is another way. The Church can be a spiritual resource peculiarly suited to the temper of most British people – morally concerned, not greatly given to intricacies of dogma, not making claims to an exclusive monopoly of truth, yet deeply aware of a spiritual depth to life.

One may thus draw a contrast between the magisterial church and the ministerial church. The magisterial Church seeks to lay down the law for the whole population; to support a State structure of Christian laws and to require acceptance of its doctrines for participation in public office. The ministerial Church seeks to provide resources for personal vision and transformation, but within a wider context which permits a variety of personal quests for religious meaning. In this sense, the religious environment will be essentially plural. The problem of such a pluralist view is that there may be thousands of faiths and sects and none of them may have much influence on national life. Is there not a danger that a state without religion will become wholly areligious and thus reduce religion to insignificance? It may be thought better to have a tolerant, morally sensitive and intellectually critical religion than to have none. If so, one can have a Christian State, not in the sense of imposing one set of moral and ideological rules on all its members, but in the sense that there is a national institutional base for the expression of the basic beliefs and values which have historically formed a society and which still command the respect of the great majority of its members.

The idea of a Christian State in the strong or magisterial sense is a contradiction of the primal Christian insight that all persons must be respected and loved, that their beliefs must therefore be taken seriously and that God may speak to us through the beliefs of others as they disclose limitations of ignorance, partiality and intolerance in ourselves. But the idea of a Christian State in the weak or ministerial sense can be a highly desirable means of expressing shared values and symbols, a resource from which people might draw strength and guidance, and a means of formulating a social vision of justice and peace founded on more than mere human convenience or desire. It is a good thing to have a religion established by law as long as most members of a state take religious questions seriously, as long as dissent is permitted, as long as the established religion is concerned to encourage constructive conversations with other religious communities, to permit diversity of interpretation within itself and to show a concern to formulate a broad value base for the state as a whole. If that is so, Britain can be a liberal state, guarding and encouraging human freedom, a tolerant state, permitting many faiths freedom of expression, but not a secular state, regarding religion just as a matter of private preference.

A certain sort of religious tradition may justifiably be established by law. Whether the people want any religion so established or whether the Church of England is such a religion are questions which may be properly raised. So far as I can see, the answer at present would be affirmative, and I would like to encourage attempts to see that they remain so. For, in the end, all social values stand on a religious foundation. That foundation has certainly been shaken in Britain since the seventeenth century. Unless it can be securely underpinned, or perhaps renewed to take account of the upheavals that have taken place, it will be very difficult to assure ourselves that there is a human and worthwhile future to look forward to. It may be hard for religious believers to tread the narrow path between retreating into a citadel of conviction in opposition to the wider culture and accepting all beliefs with indifference as matters of personal taste. But that narrow path must be maintained if religion is to be a basis for moral and social values. If it can be, then the idea of a liberal Christian State may be seen, not as a weakening of ancient belief, but as a clearer articulation of its own deepest commitments and as an appropriate expression of the idea of a Christian culture.

2 Christian Politics in a Society of Plural Values
Edward Norman

There are no absolute relationships of church and state, of religion and politics, and perhaps no ideal ones either. The configuration of influences which determines the political and social culture of nations in any particular moment of their development will itself suggest the kinds of relationships that they will find appropriate, or may seem to them to be correct local representations of universally true models. In Byzantine experience – the most complete attempt in Christian history at an earthly embodiment of the heavenly society – Christ and his saints, in the spacial symbolism of the Pantocrator, descended to the world, and right order and religious belief became co-extensive. The Kingdom of Christ, and citizenship in the societies of men, were then recognized as being of the same nature. Limited to the conditions and ideas of its time and place, the Byzantine model seems plainly unsuited to the world as it now is. It was, as it happens, not even compatible with the realities of its own time, though contemporaries were unable to appreciate by just how much: the corrupting consequences of human nature, and the instability of human social and cultural contrivances, are not promising materials for the construction of a celestial city. But the notion that religious identity is collective, that a people or a social group adopt religious belief as a unit and require a government that corresponds to it, has guaranteed the 'Christendom' model a long history. A high degree of uniformity is necessary for such a polity, however, and government needs the confidence and the ideological certainty to enforce its sacral convictions in very material ways. That confidence, and the conditions in which it may be exercised, are largely absent from modern Western societies.

Yet not all traces of the 'Christendom' model have vanished, and surviving ones, in secularized forms, are still regarded by many people as essential to good government. First of these, and in practice incorporating most others, is the conviction that government must serve grand, righteous ends. Political organization no longer represents heaven upon earth, but it is required to prescribe certain ideals which, laid out as a polity, amount to the institutional embodiment of a view of humanity and its

17

ethical and material needs. Thus the sacral qualities of the modern world, as secular icons, are made tests of good government – democracy, collectivist social welfare, racial equality, and a quite detailed checklist of benefits and rights without which governments are thought to be inadequately responsive to the legitimate aspirations of their constituents. The problem for the purpose of analysis is that the resulting form of government, the liberal collectivism of the contemporary world, has an extremely insistent moral basis but no agreed moral identity. No one is really able to describe what is the moral idea, or the ultimate philosophical reference, of which the structure of government is a representation. As a convenient substitute there is much talk of 'human rights', but these, like most natural law formulations, lack a stable content. Their very generality gives them an appeal: everyone can subscribe to noble and removed aspirations precisely because they exist as a series of ideal tableaux. Attempts to embody them in the real world encounter immediate controversy, especially between the understandings of different nations or social classes.

May the ethical basis of contemporary liberal government be said to be religious in any practical sense? Is there reference to any explicit creed or institutional authority, that is to say? There does not appear to be, at any rate in Western societies, and the existence of a diversity of religious beliefs, or the absence of them, in most Western societies, hardly encourages the idea of divine law as the ultimate reference of the state, despite surviving deposits of the former Christian confessionalism which lie scattered around the Western political landscape. In effect, much of the justification of modern liberal democracy is rendered in terms of a kind of calculated hedonism. People are obliged by law to collective benevolence because they will themselves become beneficiaries of it. Human equality is to be accorded exact political expression because past experience of systems from which it was absent now constitute the demonology of the democrats. Nobody, however, cares to give a name or a philosophical pedigree to the ultimate sanction of modern human association. Some suppose there is none; but that agreeable scepticism is rare, and perhaps a majority imagine that the rhetoric of human rights is self-authenticating. These truths, as the American Founding Fathers declared, are 'self-evident'.

In reality, this convenient avoidance of identifying the philosophical basis of the morality of government raises some awkward theoretical issues. Liberal government is very properly concerned with the acceptance of value pluralism in society. After three millennia of thought and speculation about the nature of political association, men and women have not been able to agree. That is why the existing arrangements are left nameless. The disagreement actually indicates a considerable maturity. Despite the traces of the 'Christendom' model – the attempt to make political society correspond exactly to a unitary version of the purposes of life – public figures today are prepared as never before to acknowledge the legitimate presence of divergent views about the moral foundations. This is, it is true, not tolerated in relation to a number of sacral values, like democracy or equality, but it is allowed over such matters as personal life-styles, sexual orientation, or religious belief. These types of thing, reserved to the judgement of the individual, are very important and were seen to be so in traditional society, which accordingly regulated them. They are sometimes more important than the leading sacral values, regulated by the liberal governments of today, precisely because they affect the individual much more directly, and engage emotional consciousness more immediately, than the large declarations in which the leading sacral values are expressed. Liberal government has become an exercise in enlightened exclusion. The State legislates the details of applied sacral issues, as in law, for example, about the use of the fiscal system to achieve social welfare provisions, and it denies its own entry into such areas of 'private morality' as, for example, adult sexuality or religious observance. In Britain, of course, there are numerous legal and constitutional survivals from the past, when the official establishments of religion had their ethical teachings explicitly embodied in law. These are highly formal, however, and although particular sectional interests occasionally try to breathe new life into them they are plainly anomalies. Modern liberal government is about how best to exclude certain areas of morality and belief from its own sovereignty while at the same securing a balance of interests in society at large. It is John Stuart Mill's classic dilemma of attempting to distinguish between actions which concern only the individual and actions which affect society; and the theoretical problems which he encountered over operating a political system of exclusions remain unresolved. A government which accepts as its role the presidency over a society of legitimately competing values is thus a government with diminished functions. The old confessional State saw its duty as upholding Christian truth; the liberal State must leave questions of ultimate truth, as well as many details of the citizens' life-styles, to the determination of individual choice. At the same time, and sometimes inconsistently, the liberal State upholds collectivist 'truth', and is very prescriptive about the provision of welfare – using the power and agencies of the State to propagate and enforce moral positions in relation to human claims to material benefits. So the modern State both does, and does not, concern itself with questions of ultimate moral value.

If contemporary Christians endorse the notion of excluding the State from interference in the capacity of citizens to choose their own values and beliefs – and evidently most of the leadership of Christian opinion does – they will logically recognize that the use of the power of the State to propagate religious truth and morality is questionable. In a society of plural values, privatising religion is one of the first requirements, and the historical record certainly shows that to have been the case in Britain. The relative separation of Church and State in the nineteenth century took place precisely because a still largely Christian political society recognized the existence of competing religious denominations, and saw it as an injustice for one version of Christianity to be preferred by the State above others. An anomalous State Church actually survived, at least in two of the four constituent parts of the United Kingdom, but virtually all of the public significance of the Anglican Church in England and the Presbyterian Church in Scotland was removed from the statute book by repealing laws which gave them exclusive legal protection. In today's world, political leaders only very rarely show any preparedness to consult the established Church over matters of public policy. This occurs in matrimonial law or education, where the Church has an historical function, and even then the Church is only one among a number of institutions and sectional interests whose views are sought out. The established Church itself increasingly behaves as an external critic of government, and operates as a social pressure-group. It seems, if anything, to be relieved at surrendering its former moral pre-eminence in the halls of power. This, in turn, helps to give reality to the existence of a society of plural values. In that sense the privatisation of religion – vehemently resisted by the nineteenth-century established Church – ought to be attractive to the Church leaderships of the present time, and for good reason, since however much they lament an understanding of Christianity which denies its formal role in public affairs they are unwilling to see themselves as part of the machinery of the State.

The practice of democracy is only compatible with the existence of a legal connection of Church and State, of religious opinion and public life, where the state has excluded very large areas of individual choice from its competency. And having excluded them there is then no need for the State to use the Church or Christianity as the agency of values. For who can suppose that morality, and questions about ultimate values, may properly be determined by the counting of heads? The modern indication that they are not chosen in this way is that political choice is generally restricted in practice to material issues: general elections are fought primarily on matters related to the economy. It is a habit that the east European countries newly released from communism (which was, paradoxically, all ideas and insufficiently expert at economic management) are rapidly picking up from the West. After initial outpourings of high principle, they are absorbing themselves with economic questions. When the modern liberal state has excluded itself, because of its own incompetence in such matters, from 'higher' moral and spiritual matters it is bound to become an affair of shop management. The result is distasteful, necessary, and ideologically correct; politicians themselves, reluctant to abdicate from the thrones of moral discernment, continue to employ the verbal apparatus of high principle to describe the purposes of their essential bookkeeping. Are the churches qualified to offer opinions about the material management of the State, which is now the primary function of modern government?

It is equally clear that the qualifications possessed by politicians to get involved with religious belief may be questioned. Unlettered in the categories of doctrinal construction, and prone to superficiality when it comes to the mysterious and ambiguous operations of divine grace, politicians usually only employ religion as part of a general appeal to be themselves recognised as custodians of the 'high moral ground'. Some readily advance from this relatively benign state of affairs to the much more potentially sinister enterprise of seeking to justify their political conduct by reference to the sanctions of religion. Then it becomes evident that by religion they actually mean such matters as family values, or the need for morality as a corrective to crime, or some principled rationale behind a redistribution of wealth. The tendency to replace spirituality with ethicism as the centre of religious understanding – already plainly evident within the leadership of the Church itself – is greatly enhanced by the politicians when they envisage Christian values as the basis of their own material management of the State. This is all very much a fringe phenomenon, however. Appeals to religion by political figures are episodic and exceptional; most keep discreetly quiet about their religious convictions, or lack of them, presumably fearful of upsetting one section of the electorate by associating with another. How many politicians mention their religious allegiance in their election manifestos, when appealing to the voters to judge their worth for public office? How many voters expect them to? The secularization of the political order is very advanced.

These observations relate largely to Britain and to Western liberal societies at the present time. In such locations, the involvement of the Churches in the political process will be as dimensions of an overall value pluralism. They are among a number of competing moral and spiritual agencies or beliefs. The Churches themselves, as good liberals, would probably want it no other way. They now see themselves as witnesses to certain truths and to moral values which they can hold up for public judgement, as the bearers of critiques of public policy. They probably no longer envisage a 'Christendom' policy, in which Christian agencies seek the establishment of a state structure intended to embody Christian truth. Their acceptance of a pluralism of moral values in society is both realistic and in accordance with the expectations of the other social components. Like the other components, of course, the Churches inconsistently rush to endorse the use of the power of the State to enshrine matters of social morality: the secularized 'Christendom' model is the collectivist welfare machinery of the modern State, which has the very articulate support of the Churches. All this, however, leaves the problem of the moral identity of the State unresolved; in the end it is an extremely vague moral pedigree which allows the sanction of law to operate. Do Christians support welfare collectivism because they wish to embody Christianity in law, and use the power of the State to enforce it? Do Christians campaign for laws on environmental issues because their ideas about the stewardship of the world should be enforced because they are Christian? Do Christians wish to leave individuals free of state control over the details of religious belief because that is a Christian thing to do? These are matters which are left very imprecisely labelled. At the present time the moral incoherence at the centre of political association does not appear to project the problem into public consciousness. Recent exchanges in the British parliament about the religious provisions of education legislation – about the extent to which teaching in the state schools should be explicitly Christian – seemed to suggest that a majority persisted in claiming a religious identity at the centre of the political constitution. Comparable evidences occasionally surface over other 'moral' issues, relating to marriage law, sexual conduct, Sabbath observance, or medical ethics. In reality, however, it is doubtful if this all amounts to very much, and there are no signs, despite the clamours of some influential pressure-groups, that either the Churches or the State are contemplating the use of the machinery of the State to construct a new confessional Christian society.

But how stable is the liberal society of plural values? Since it is the nature of political arrangements in the modern world to be more fragile than they usually appear, it is clearly right to question the durability of liberal values. Are we are present in a highly untypical interlude, following the demise of traditional society with its unitary moral base and its social control, and before the reappearance of new controlled societies, to be set up as embodiments of vigorously assembled ideologies? The spread of mass education may provide a pointer. On the one hand, it is intended as a way of introducing the widest possible range of people to the insights of critical thought, and so can be seen as a reinforcement of liberal values; on the other, it encourages the notion that the ills of human society may be corrected by discernible programmes which can be furthered by political means. In one sense it makes for a kind of individual anarchy, where each person regards the fruits of his thinking as sovereign; in another it tends to foster mass support for ideals which are held out as packaged explanations of social and moral phenomena. The real tyrannies are the tyrannies of the mind. Some of the most controlled societies of the twentieth century have been reared upon the democratic assent of mass electorates. Beyond liberal pluralism there could well lie a future world of benign totalitarianism supported by public opinion. There is no way of telling.

These speculations would be idle indeed but for the prospect they offer of clarifying the position of religion in relation to government. In the realm of liberal pluralism, with its limited view of the legitimate capacity of the State, the Churches are able to participate with the other components easily enough. The conventions which protect the various parts of the pluralism also protect them. What religious bodies should ask of any state structure, in the first instance, is not whether it envolves or embodies some grand moral or philosophical design but whether it allows space and freedom for the practice and transmission of religious belief. In a society of plural values, with a liberal polity, the Churches may surely claim all they need on that account. The State, for its part, should pursue, as far as it can, a neutral course between the competing moralisms. That is, as already noticed, only achieved by a reduction of its authority. There will of course be many ways in which the State will act in the light of moral considerations; these, however, will remain, as they now are, necessarily incoherent. The rhetoric of Human Rights will fill up the gaps. It is an imperfect situation and, from the point of view of the ideologically fastidious, extremely unideal. But it has the advantage of preserving freedom and diversity – for the time being. All acts of government in the end rest on moral sanction for their legitimacy, and ours is increasingly a society of compulsive moralism. So the ingredients are unstable. What if the state is pushed by one of the components of the pluralism, which may chance to have an electoral majority at the time, into the promotion of a single ideology – whether overall, or touching some aspect of the national life? What if the State then exchanges its neutrality, wholly or in part, for commitment to an incorporative moral position? What if it should slide out of neutrality and into a militant secularism? The Churches and other religious agencies could scarcely relish the possibility of a State structure which intended the use of the influence of government for the promotion of a rigorously secular frame of moral reference for society. Some will argue that this already happens over particulars, as, for example, in legislative attitudes to medical ethics.

In its simplest formulation, the question in such conditions then becomes: why should the Churches, by holding themselves back from active participation in the political process, allow their ideological rivals or opponents to conduct the management of the State? Why should they hand over the means by which the moral environment is created to those with whom they may differ? The great threat to mankind today, from a Christian perspective, does not derive from a nuclear exchange, or some ecological catastrophe, but from the advance of materialism. By this is meant not the absorption of the person in material possessions or distractions, but serious philosophical materialism – the interpretation of human life as a product of material processes, the lives of men and women divorced from transcendence, their sensations believed to be the consequence of material conditioning screened through layers of human culture. This threat, both in vulgarized and in sophisticated ideological renditions, is plentifully to hand in the modern world. Until just recently it seemed to come from Marxism; its real danger is now more insidious, however, for it emerges from an unconscious orientation of life and thought almost universally encountered in Western liberal societies. Christians know that what we *are* in some measure actually does reflect the conditioning of circumstance, especially in early years and through education. Hence the importance attached in traditional societies to creating and sustaining a Christian State structure, one in which individuals would be reared and socialised in the context of Christian values. And hence, of course, the 'Christendom' model.

The experience of human societies suggests a permanent competition of ideologies, each one of which needs brute confidence to embody its beliefs, and especially its view of man, in institutional forms which reach up to the power of the State itself in order to secure continuity and survival. In traditional society, again, essential values and religious belief were derived collectively: a whole people, or a whole social unit, was identifiable by its profession of a single religion. The adoption of a religious identity was not an individual enterprise, as in modern liberal society, but a matter of accepting the values and world-outlook of a social group. It is very properly regarded as an advance in human experience that collective religious enforcement has been abandoned. It was one of the great features of religion as taught by Christ that men and women were called individually to the way of salvation. The Jewish religion, which he came to reform, was collective. It took many centuries for the individualising of religious vocation to receive full expression in the world, and it only really came with the breakup of traditional society. The consequential beginnings of the privatising of religion, which is a feature of the atomized structure of liberal society, has left Christians ill-equipped to defend their beliefs in the attrition of competitive values. Once religion has become a matter of private option it loses its utility as a means of social control, and so the State is less and less concerned with it. Historically, at any rate in Britain, the effects of the privatising of religion through the breakup of traditional society occurred at the same time as the recognition that society was becoming characterized by religious pluralism: the two, indeed, were linked. When the political pressures of religious dissent successfully sought a reduction of the influence of the established Church, in the nineteenth century, they had no wish to weaken the relationship between law and Christian values, but their campaign over the constitutional position of the state Church, together with the wider cultural and intellectual emancipation of sections of the intelligentsia from allegiance to Christian belief, resulted, as is well known, in the establishment of the liberal polity. It happened pragmatically, in a series of claims to simple justice. In the United States, on the other hand, the separation of Church and State was enshrined in the Federal Constitution and spread over time to the various states of the Union. There, too, however, there was no intention of weakening the relationship of Christianity and public life, or of diminishing the essentially Christian basis of law. In practice, that has tended to happen because, in the present century, liberal interpretation of Constitutional rights has required it. As in Britain, no agreed alternative philosophical basis of public life was proposed. The experience of both these nations shows just how difficult it is to arrive at a moral basis for law which is not still popularly taken to be in some sense Christian, or, to put it the other way round, how no agreed alternative to Christian morality has actually emerged as the sanction of public association. Yet in neither country, despite that, do governments today seek to use the power of the State or the rule of law to create a Christian society. Recent indications of a 'return to traditional values' in Republican America and Conservative Britain have sometimes hinted at Christian values, and even claimed them explicitly – as in the search of

the leadership of the British Conservative Party for a Christian justification of market economics – but no serious political will exists which
would attempt the resuscitation of Christendom.

In both the experience of political development, therefore, and in the
values of contemporary liberalism, there is little to favour a systematic
connection of public polity and the doctrines of the Church. The main
Christian bodies, for their part, have no inclination to differ from that
assessment, except over one or two specific issues: the recent attitude of
the British Churches to the preservation of sabbatarian legislation, for
example, and even here the motive cannot really have been a desire to
return to the force of law to protect Christian practices. It must have
derived from political unease with the general policies of the government, with their emphasis on market influences, which the issue of
Sunday trading appeared to symbolise. In this, and in other examples, the
Churches have clearly not thought through the logical constitutional
implications of their position. Christian leaders in general recognise that
the days when they could expect the power of the State to propagate their
teachings are over. They presumably also see that the main occasions
for the transmission of religious truth are to be located in the family and
in the institutional operations of the Church itself. Among the latter are
church schools and charitable enterprises. In the circumstances of democratic liberal pluralism, with the diminished functions of the State which
are annexed to it – at least over what is left after the welfare and economic collectivist powers of the State have taken their lion's share – the
Church should see its political role as like that of other components of
the pluralism: to protect itself from improper encroachments by the State,
and to regulate its relationship to other elements within the pluralism. It
should also be concerned with the general critique of public issues and
public life – with the acts of government viewed from Christian perspectives. It is unlikely there will ever be agreement within the Christian
body itself about precisely how those perspectives will be defined or
categorized, or any agreement, come to that, between the State and the
Church about the legitimate sphere of either. Discussion and disagreement over the mutual relationship of morality and politics are the ever-
lasting stuff of public life. What the Church should *not* be doing, while
the liberal pluralism exists, is to attempt to use the power of the State
to assemble a visible Christian society in the world – at least as long as
all the other components of the pluralism reserve their own spheres as
well. For the Church to seek a unilateral reversion to the 'Christendom'
model would, in prevailing circumstances, produce injustice for those
who are outside its allegiance and would, anyway, elicit extremely mixed

consequences. Whether or not Christian values have a majority assent in society is hardly pertinent to this: since it is not accepted that truth can be arrived at by democratic process the possibility that, at a given moment, the Church may express the popular mind is not authority for using the force of law to attempt the structural establishment of the Kingdom of Christ, in whole or in part. There are, for example, those who contend that this is not a plural society at all, because a silent majority still subscribe to Christian moral values; and there are others who question the extent to which secularization is as solid a phenomenon as it appears to be. These are not relevant considerations. Pluralism of values should not be defined in numerical but in qualitative terms. It exists, as Mill used to argue, where educated opinion is divided within itself, and it exists within contemporary Western societies.

It was suggested at the outset that there were no absolutes or permanently fixed markers in determining the relationship of Christianity and political experience. The acceptance of liberal pluralism seems appropriate in prevailing circumstances, with the consequent implications for a limited participation by religious agencies in the direction of the moral basis of the State. Should liberal society be superseded by more unitary controlled political arrangements, however, or perhaps in existing societies which lack liberal safeguards, it may surely be necessary for religious bodies to defend their existence by resort to the machinery of the State (where they are capable of doing so) if this will prevent assault by alien ideology. Such a situation would occur in the breakup of a liberal polity. Then the Christian leadership could properly contemplate either an attempt at the restoration of the pluralism – hardly likely to succeed, however, in conditions where it had just broken down – or something like a return to the 'Christendom' model, rather than allow an unchallenged occupation of political power by an ideological adversary. In either case, however, experience is likely to show that divergencies within the Churches themselves about the nature of political action will scarcely be less than the differences between themselves and their ideological opponents. Only in the odd worst-case scenario are the issues involved likely to achieve consensus within the Churches themselves. For the internal secularization of Christianity, as the Churches have progressively accommodated to the social and cultural values of contemporary society, has reduced its capability of eliciting uniquely religious responses to the conduct of human society. When the Churches in the modern world have found themselves in opposition to particular political beliefs or practices it has usually been because they share values found elsewhere in the available political spectrum – not because they are directing light that has come from another dimension of experience altogether. What is unique about Christianity is revealed truth, and that has to do with the forgiveness of sin and the possibility of salvation. It is not about enforcing its beliefs with the power of the State. It is not about the conduct of government, unless the intention, as in Byzantium, really is the creation of heaven on earth.

3 Religion, War and the Gulf
Tony Benn

Anyone who doubts the power of religion has only got to be reminded of the famous question posed by Stalin, 'How many battalions does the Pope have?' He got his answer quite soon. Bush might well ask, 'How many battalions does the Prophet Muhammad have?' because we are talking about matters where religious interest and feeling are very strong.

I was elected to Parliament on 30 November 1950. On that very day, when I was busy campaigning, President Truman announced, almost casually, that he might use an atom bomb on China. That was at the time of the Korean War and I wonder how much has changed over the years.

Martin Buber, the theologian, whom I once had the honour to meet in Tel-Aviv, said that everything was really a choice between propaganda and education, and I take that view too. My fear about the way serious, indeed fundamental, issues are dealt with is that media coverage is so shallow. We get a lot of experts on television but there is not a great deal of depth. There is no attempt either to understand the historical perspective or have some vision of the future. Harold Wilson once said, 'A week is a long time in politics', but I prefer Mao Tse-tung's comment when asked what influence he thought the French Revolution had had on world history. Mao replied, 'It's a little too soon to say.'

Religious broadcasts are the only programmes in which it is now possible to have a serious political discussion because most of the current affairs programmes are looking for the 'sound bite'. They interview you for twenty-five minutes and one sentence is picked out by the producer. Politics has become a spectator sport in which *Newsnight*, with its computers, tells viewers that on the basis of a by-election in Wigan, David Owen will form a majority government. The media has now got as great a control of public life as the Church had in medieval times. For those who wonder, as I often have, whether God or Mammon is what we worship, the answer comes from Dominic Harrod who will tell you on the *Financial World Tonight* what has happened to the pound sterling to three decimal points against a basket of European currencies. And on the basis of what has happened to the pound sterling, a hospital is closed, or interest rates increased.

This whole new school of politics is built up by the media who declare that public meetings, the discussion of the kind we are having tonight, are defunct. I have great arguments in the National Executive Committee of the Labour Party as to whether public meetings are worth having. 'What's the point of addressing the faithful?' I am asked. I reply that the Church would be unlikely to have survived 2000 years if it hadn't addressed the faithful every Sunday. If the Pope had had to rely on the odd photo-opportunity created by a miracle at Lourdes, the Catholic Church would have been unlikely to have thrived.

What I am about to say is not a party political broadcast for the Labour Party. How could it be? The leadership it has given since the Gulf War has been, in my judgement, wholly failing. Nor is it a sermon. I, who have no religious qualifications, could hardly do that in the Chapter House of Canterbury Cathedral.

What I *would* like to do is to explore some of the moral choices that now face us, and lie ahead in respect of the Gulf and the Middle East.

The conclusion I have come to in the course of my life is that politics and religion are basically the same thing. I know there is a view on the left that 'religion is the opium of the people', the famous phrase of Karl Marx, and that life began when socialism was born. But I have never taken that view. I think that those who deny that the great political arguments of earlier centuries were fought in the name of religion fail to understand the history from which we ourselves have come. Some of our greatest political rights have been won in the name of religion. The Reformation was a theological upheaval but it also of course meant a break with the power of Rome, a political decision.

Henry VIII created our oldest nationalised industry, the Church of England, because he wanted priests in every pulpit in every parish on every Sunday telling the people that God wanted them to do what the King wanted them to do. That was why the Church of England was nationalised. And, as I discovered when I was Postmaster General, Charles II set up the nationalised Royal Mail because he wanted to open everybody's letters and that was the only way of doing it. The Conservative Party nationalised the BBC because it wanted a pundit on every channel every night announcing that there was no alternative to what the Government wanted.

So the relationship between religion and politics is a very close one. Certainly faith lies at the root of religion and faith lies at the root of many political convictions – and of course there is a very close connection between religious faith and political commitment, though not in some crude link with a political party.

Both Churches and political parties create structures in order to survive and once a structure and a hierarchy are in place, that hierarchy is as interested in maintaining its own power as it is in propagating the faith that brought it into being. The Church of England has bishops, the Labour Party has regional organisers and historically bishops and regional organisers have spent more time fighting heretics than they have in perpetuating Christianity or socialism.

This relationship between faith and structure is something I was taught as a child, having been brought up on the Old Testament: the conflict between the kings and the prophets, the kings who exercised power and the prophets who preached righteousness. The tension between the flame of faith and the structure of power is to be found in every society. And structures can go wrong.

One of the ways in which the Christian Church over the centuries has, in my opinion, failed in its duty is that it forgot that the brotherhood and sisterhood of men and women is something that has an element of 'here and now' about it. Bishops sometimes say to the rich 'If only you are kind,' and to the poor, 'If only you are patient, it will be all right when you are dead', but people say, 'We want social justice now.' There is an exact political parallel in the Labour Party which says, 'If only you keep your head down and your options open, things will be all right when there is a Labour Government.' I think that the 'here and now' of social responsibility is actually the fuel of the engine that brings social justice.

There are broadly four levels in politics. The level that receives the most attention is of the personality: who leads what parties. I happen to think leaders are totally disposable. Some may leave footprints in the sands of time if they are also teachers but those who have simply held office may leave no impression whatever on the period of history through which they are living and leaders change, as we have seen quite recently.

At a deeper level comes policy. Policies change with circumstances. In wartime, for example, cost is no object. In peacetime – we are told – everything has to be measured according to its cost. I think a lot of people looking at the Gulf War will be asking themselves, for example, how it is possible to spend millions a day to house the troops in Saudi Arabia when we can't afford to house the homeless in London. How is it that we can spend, I think, something like £500 billion – which will be the cost of the war including the £200 billion on the destruction of Iraq – when 27 million people in Africa are facing famine within a matter of weeks. How do you justify it? In short, priorities change. More fundamental than policies are institutions – who decides what we do. Institutions have a duration that goes beyond the immediate system and describes the difference between a dicatorship and a democracy.

But the foundation of politics must be moral in character. A society must make up its mind whether it wishes to be a community or a jungle. If you feel, as Christians and socialists should, that we are all part of a family whether we live in Baghdad or in Canterbury or in Africa, this will dispose you towards certain policies.

Although there is an enormous, indeed absolutely unbridgeable theological gulf between those who believe that the brotherhood and sisterhood of men and women derives from the fatherhood of God, and those who believe that we are brothers and sisters anyway, the ethics of the responsible humanist or the responsible Christian or the responsible Jew or the responsible Muslim, are often extraordinarily similar. The ethics of a society, from wherever they derive, will give you some clue as to how moral questions are to be resolved.

Now, can I turn to the question of the Gulf War and put forward my conviction that the duty to save life is a duty deriving from the belief that we are all brothers and sisters. This came out most vividly, I thought, in the last two or three days when the beaten Iraqi army, withdrawing from Kuwait, was pursued by aircraft and bombers. The B52s were bombing ahead to crater the road so that there was no escape and these wretched conscripts were fried alive in their tanks. I thought that was *wrong*. The bombing of Baghdad, the heaviest raid of the war, occurred yesterday morning when it was clear the war was over.

More generally, throughout the whole of this conflict, the question of whether we should kill or whether we should talk, whether we should negotiate or whether we should destroy, has lain at the heart of the political decisions that had to be made. These are moral questions.

I have noticed – and I am sure everybody has, whatever view they take of the war – that in order to justify the killing, the enemy has to be dehumanised. The language used has not referred to casualties but to targets. There has been a hi-tech war with Jaguars with TRX computers and LSV laser-finding bombsights which seem to kill nobody. That dehumanisation is a necessary part of the process of war, that the enemy ceases to be human. Some of the popular press glories in war in a way that has really frightened me because of the impact this has upon *our* society. It is hard at the moment to estimate how many people have been killed. The Iraqi Red Crescent has told Ramsay Clarke, former Attorney General of the United States, who was in Baghdad and Basra a few weeks ago, that probably 20 000 people had been killed. The figures that the Saudi military authorities gave the *Washington Post* today spoke of between 85 000 and 100 000 Iraqi soldiers having been killed or injured – conscripts, of course, most of them. The World Health Organization, which has been in Baghdad, says babies are dying of cholera and dysentery and diarrhoea because there is no clean water supply. The damage done to Iraq is calculated to be £200 billion and some people in the United States have spoken of bombing the country back into the Stone Age. War is a horrible thing. But I think the characteristic which is most concerning from a moral point of view, is that these facts and figures are concealed in the presentation of the war.

The second moral duty to come out of a situation like this is the duty to understand. There are some people who make it seem very complex: 'If you knew what I knew, you wouldn't ask that silly question.' There are other people who oversimplify. But it seems to me that those in a representative capacity – and I don't mean just an elected MP, or the bishop, or anyone else – have a duty to unravel, to clarify, to explain. To do that we really do have to have some historical background.

I am not a scholar but I have always studied the historical background of all problems in order to try and make sense of them. I have tried to study the relations between the West and the Middle East during this crisis.

I was in Algiers a year or two ago and I met a former Egyptian Foreign Minister who told me he had been to a seminar in Cairo about the Crusades, in which, of course, Richard Coeur de Lion, whose statue stands outside the House of Commons, fought Saladin in order to capture the holy places. I asked what he had learned. 'Oh,' he said, 'We discovered that the European arms manufacturers were selling weapons to Richard Coeur de Lion *and* to Saladin!' That was a powerful reminder that the arms trade doesn't change.

Then, an American architect who writes to me from time to time, sent me this week an Instruction from Pope Innocent III to the Doge of Venice in 1198 saying that any Christian who supplied arms to or traded with Mohammedans would be excommunicated. Christian sanctions against the Muslims! One of the things I fear most is the racism and anti-Muslim feeling that has been stimulated as a part of the war even though we are reminded that most of the Arab world has been on the side of the coalition.

Coming forward to the nineteenth century, in 1877, which is not so very long ago, the Russian army moved towards Turkey and Queen Victoria sent a task force to the Dardanelles. At the time, somebody wrote a little verse, which you may have heard.

We don't want to fight, but by jingo if we do
We've got the ships, we've got the men, we've got the money too.

Jingoism was born out of a Middle Eastern crisis not so very different
from the one we have now, and of course jingoism is what we have
been experiencing.

Imperialism! The word 'imperialism' is now regarded as a rather controversial one to use but if you read Joe Chamberlain in the nineteenth
century, imperialism was the white man's burden. He had a Christian
duty to bring the natives to a knowledge of Christianity. 'Trade follows
the Cross.' The missionary went first, then the traders arrived. That was
imperialism. In 1897 when my mother, who is ninety-four, was born, the
world was run by three men – the King of England, the Kaiser of Germany,
and the Tsar of Russia and they were all Queen Victoria's grandsons.
(I *think* the Tsar married Queen Victoria's granddaughter.)

Remember that the Turkish Empire broke up after the First World
War, and because Kuwait was an oil-rich province and it was convenient
to have it under our control, the frontier between Kuwait and Iraq was
drawn up by a British official, Sir Percy Cox. In 1920, when Britain
was trying to subdue Iraq, a man called Harris, an RAF squadron
leader, came up with the idea of bombing the area, and mustard gas
was used by the Royal Air Force. Nine thousand tribesmen were killed
in that uprising. Of course, Harris became famous as Air Marshal
'Bomber' Harris who obliterated Dresden during the last World War.

In 1958, Selwyn Lloyd, who was Foreign Secretary, wrote to Foster
Dulles, US Secretary of State, and told him Britain was going to occupy
Kuwait and turn it into a Crown colony because we needed the oil.
Foster Dulles replied, 'What a very good idea.'

So a little history gives you a different perspective on what we have
been taught about our enduring duty to protect people from aggression
and chemical weapons. The West has supported Saddam. Only three
years ago there was a Baghdad Arms Fair organised by the British government. There is another international arms fair in Birmingham this summer
and I am sure it will be busy because there will be a lot of weapons that
will need to be replaced. Ten months ago, the British Government
provided £1 billion in loans for Saddam Hussein after he had used
chemical weapons on the Kurds, no doubt much of that money being
spent on buying the weapons to fight our own people.

The duty to understand is very disturbing. It disturbs the simplicities
of the battle. But it is moral duty to learn and teach and I believe that
is something we have been denied during this conflict.

I have never quite believed the goodies and baddies theory, the cow-
boy and Indian theory, for a variety of reasons, one of which is that some
of yesterday's baddies are now goodies. President Assad of Syria, who is

supposed to have been responsible for the Lockerbie bombing, is now one of our closest allies in the coalition. President Reagan invaded Grenada and President Bush went into Panama and 2000 people were killed. The Americans fought the Vietnam War in which two million people were killed and chemical weapons – Agent Orange – were used.

It is necessary to look at the interests at work. The arms manufacturers make millions out of war, and they are able to test their weapons. Every scientist in the world working on weapons research will be looking to see what was most successful in Kuwait and Iraq, just as the Exocet missile, which sank the *Sheffield* at the time of the Falklands War, is now in every army in the world. Contractors are queueing up now in order to get the contracts to rebuild Kuwait and Iraq which we have just finished destroying. The military want their budgets protected because when the Cold War came to an end they didn't know how to justify the enormous expenditure.

In this century, humanity has re-equipped itself with a completely new set of tools – killing machines, travelling machines, calculating machines, communicating machines. How is the lethal power of modern society to be controlled? I have developed five questions about democracy in the course of my political life which I ask powerful people. What power have you got? Where did you get it from? In whose interest do you exercise it? To whom are you accountable? And how can we get rid of you? These are the basic questions of democracy – how do you get rid of people who have power and make them accountable?

The United Nations was, after all, set up to 'lift from humanity the scourge of war'; those were the words of the Charter and I find it hard to believe that a war under the UN aegis proves how effective the UN is. All war is a failure of diplomacy and the UN should be viewed in terms of how it should operate. President Bush speaks of a new world order which I think really means American power harnessing the Security Council for its own ends. It is the old imperialism. Others think, and I am certainly of that view, that the United Nations should be a Parliament of humanity where people can bring the injustices from which they suffer to the attention of the world and get them resolved. That's how the Anti-Colonial Movement was brought to fruition, under the aegis of the UN.

I personally think that the veto of a superpower in the Security Council (and America has used it sixty-nine times, more than anybody else since 1950) should be able to be overridden by the General Assembly which represents the people of the world. And just as we elect the European Parliament, we should elect members to the General Assembly. If there was a British constituency from which a Member might be elected to the

UN, I would certainly regard that as a more important job than that of a member of our own Parliament.

During the Gulf War and before it, we had expressions from religious leaders on the morality of the war. I think everyone will share the overwhelming sense of relief that the killing has stopped because for the last six months, we have all been subjected to the most hideous war propaganda justifying the slaughter of men, women and children who had no responsibility whatever for the invasion of Kuwait by Saddam Hussein. This conditioning has stirred up hatred and hysteria on a scale we have not seen for half a century. Some of those responsible have, regrettably, been religious leaders on both sides who have solemnly declared that the fighting has the endorsement of the Almighty. Some Muslim religious leaders have called it a *Jihad* or Holy War and some Christian bishops have called it a just war. But all have seemed to authorise the killing of human beings in the name of God or Allah.

The psychological effect of this on the values of our own society will be very profound indeed because revenge creates social conflict leading to more hatred and deaths in the future. I hope the United Nations may establish a Commission of Inquiry to examine the causes of the war, the cost of the war, the casualties, the role played by those who armed Iraq and encouraged it to invade Kuwait. The UN must look at its own role and ask why it allowed itself to be sidelined and bypassed and neutralized over so much of the period and turn its attention to the rights of the Palestinians and the Kurds, and the pursuit of human rights in the world. And particularly the urgent need to help those now facing starvation in Africa.

I hope you will allow me to express this view about the theory of the just war. Everyone has to search their conscience and reach their own conclusion but being brought up to believe in the priesthood of all believers, I cannot accept that you need a bishop to intervene between yourself and the Almighty when moral judgements have to be made. A bishop can be a teacher but a bishop cannot unilaterally amend the Ten Commandments and say, 'Thou shalt not kill, unless it is to kill Iraqis'.

I do not speak as a pacifist. I haven't the moral courage to be like those in India who were beaten down by the British troops and accepted it. I am not a pacifist in the sense that if somebody came here now with a knife and was trying to kill somebody, I would not fight back. But wisdom requires us to look carefully at the scale of all this and not try to control other people's views. The most courageous man I have met in the last six months is a young lance-bombardier who has deserted from the army on principle because he will not go to the Gulf to fight in a war which he says is wrong.

Can I finish by trying to sum up. I am personally persuaded that this crisis, which is about oil and power, could have been resolved without bloodshed.

I am frightened by the role of the media during the war. I think there will be many young people who have seen the coverage of the last few months and will conclude 'if there's a problem, kill somebody' instead of seeking to negotiate.

I fear the UN has been hijacked, and we have seen a return to imperialism. I fear this could be the first North–South war now that the East–West conflict has eased. I fear it will leave a legacy of bitterness.

These are my reasons for having opposed the war which I have done as honestly as I can. I finish by offering you a comment from Mahatma Gandhi whom I met in London when I was a child of six. A British journalist asked him, 'Mr Gandhi, what do you think of civilization in Britain?' Gandhi replied, 'I think it would be a very good idea.'

4 Christian Discipleship and Politics

John J. Vincent

TWO TYPES OF DISCIPLESHIP

Christianity has always inspired at least two basic styles of discipleship. Each of them carries with it appropriate political stances.

The first style of discipleship is basically that of the cultural insiders. This type assumes that the call of Christ is to a commitment to witness within the structures of society, belonging to its professions, seeking their good. On this model, the radical demands of discipleship are understood mainly in a moral way – that the Christian serves the existing institutions, but does so with special love, or humanity, or moral integrity.

The political force of this style of discipleship is evident. The cultural insiders see their prime responsibility as to become participants in the main hierarchies of business, education, science and government. From their position within these structures, they seek to work for change. Theologically, the doctrines of Creation, Natural Law, and the Redemption of the Secular support this style.

The political advantages of the cultural insider are manifold. The existing institutions need a moral core. They need leaders with a high sense of morality and responsibility. By having Christians in such positions, the good of society is secured. Many of my contemporaries took this route. They are now directors of education or social services, or head teachers, or senior social workers.

The political disadvantages are, however, also manifold. Once inside the system, the requirements of the system all but completely dominate. They determine the arena in which action is possible, the rules by which it has to be performed, the rewards which attend success, and the punishments which follow betrayal. Some of my contemporaries who took this route found themselves saying, 'We have sold out to the system. We are its servants, and merely oil its wheels. Apart from personal influence – which would apply wherever we were – we have achieved little in the way of change, particularly institutional change.'

The second style of Christian discipleship is that of the cultural outsiders. Here, the term 'outsider' is difficult. It is in fact hard, or even impossible, to be wholly an outsider within any society and ethos, particularly in Britain today. The ethos of our culture is too all-pervasive. We are part of it even when we attempt to escape from it. Is it better to label our second type 'alternative'? This again has problems. It makes the lines of this style of obedience totally dependent upon the straight society, to which the disciple has to be different and constantly be producing alternatives – which is unreasonable to expect. I think the best way round this difficulty is to call the second type the radical disciples. This makes the source and origin of the discipleship clear.

The political force of this stance is its coherence with the biblical tradition. The radical disciples assume that the call of Christ is the prime starting point and the ultimate appeal. Unless the disciples are literalists, they do not take every command or expectation or teaching *simpliciter*, as things to be obeyed automatically. Rather, they take them as evocative and sustaining styles and methods, which the radical disciples expect to see in action and practice in very contemporary terms, but which yet in the contemporary scene have the same basic thrusts as the original words or actions in the life and works of Jesus.

The political advantages of radical discipleship are that a stance of independence from the main structures, organisations, hierarchies and power groups is secured, and the disciples are free from the expectation of service to institutions as mediators. The disciples proceed directly from analysis of the situation, by way of evoking biblical and theological calls and antecedents, to faith-decision concerning ways to deal with the presenting situation.

Yet there are political disadvantages in being a 'radical disciple'. The stance of independence easily becomes a self-congratulatory sectarianism. Contributions which are rejected by society all too easily are assumed to be correct. Experiments within the company of disciples can prevent the politicisation of the experiments in society as a whole. Most discipleship or Christian communitarian entrepreneurs are exhausted long before they get to societal transformation. Not unnaturally, few of my contemporaries, as I recall, took this route.

A REBIRTH OF RADICAL DISCIPLESHIP

Yet for all this, radical discipleship is alive and well today – not as a way of escape, but as a way of taking the world seriously.

I believe that one of the most significant new facts of our time over the last twenty years has been the exodus of significant numbers of

Christian people from the straight society into various forms of Christian alternative society. And that means a move over, by at least a few, from the cultural insider model of discipleship to that of the radical disciple.

Most of such people have already tasted the benefits of the Great Society. They have been to colleges, universities and other places of training. They have usually had the benefits of middle-class homes, often in prosperous surroundings. They come from families of loving parents and stable relationships. They have either grown up in specifically religious or Christian environments and Churches, or have become influenced by them.

Often after university, they come to a point of negative decision. Typically, the university graduate has got hooked on a speciality without too much forethought, much less vocational reflection. At 15 or 16, they got interested in mathematics, or music, or mineralogy, possibly because of an innate hunch, more likely due to the attractions or interest of a teacher in the subject. By 17 or 18, the obvious thing is to go to university. So they spend another three or four years at their mathematics or music or mineralogy. Then, towards graduation, they go to the Careers Office. The careers officer tells them what people do with degrees in mathematics, or music or mineralogy. They look at a few options, perhaps do a few interviews. If in total confusion or doubt, they do a teachers diploma. If their mathematics or music or mineralogy leads nowhere, they can at least teach it to others!

But then a few of them 'come to themselves'. They find their chosen slot unrewarding. Then they start looking desperately for alternatives. There are alternatives in Britain today, though our straight educational system keeps the good news from most of our rising generation.

Let me tell you about one.

For nearly twenty years, we have run a 'Study Year' at the Urban Theology Unit in Sheffield. A few end up there. We ask them what they want to do. 'I don't know. The only thing I'm clear about is what I *don't* want to do. The mathematics, or music, or mineralogy.'

We find this true not only of young people. Three groups consistently emerge:

1. People who are drawn to live and work in the inner city, and need some tools, training and support with which to follow this through.
2. People who have had some experience, and need a time of 'standing back' and reflecting in the context of a Christian community of study.
3. People who are looking for a change of direction in their life and vocation, and wish to study new possibilities.

People in the first and last groups are the radical discipleship types – people in the second may be.

Typically, they come to us from doing something else after university. They are not so much discontented – though they are that – as searching. They do not want to drop out of straight society so much as drop into a real society. So for a year or two, or more, they find voluntary, part time or temporary jobs; they learn how to work in an advice centre or a youth club, or a community group or campaign. They work with the homeless, or immigrant communities, or help in schools, or with single parent families, or children in need. Or they help with clubs for old people, disabled, terminally ill, or otherwise disadvantaged.

Not very radical, you might say. Very radical indeed, I reply. For remember who these people are – the achievers of our educational system.

So I hail a rebirth of radical discipleship, in our midst, in the selfish eighties and the not yet caring nineties. I regard it as significant in terms of our society and its future. To that I will return. But first I want to argue that such radical discipleship has a theological and spiritual tradition – that it belongs to the original discipleship of the Gospels. And then I want to argue that the models of Jesus in the political situation on this day, and elements within the discipleship tradition, constitute coherent and possible stances and strategies for the disciple today.

RADICAL DISCIPLESHIP IN THE GOSPELS

The model of radical discipleship is the gospel model. In gospel times, this model was clearly differentiated from that of the cultural insider. Indeed, from the Gospels we may discern what the criteria are for a gospel alternative.

An alternative is 'something different' from the normal. In some sense, it defines itself as over against the norms. Clearly, Jesus presented and put forward an alternative in his society, an alternative represented by himself, and held up a model to be followed and repeated by other people. Even today, the Church provides a lot of things for people to do which they would not otherwise do. But are they 'valid' alternatives? The two discipleship styles are in Gospel terms:

Cultural Insider	*Radical Disciple*
1. Conformity, continuance, existing alongside God.	1. Repentance, radical change, 'turning to God'.

John J. Vincent

2. Self-justification, certainty, acting on evidence, hedging bets.	2. Faith, acting as if God exists. Trusting oneself to God.
3. Staying with existing commitments. Rich young ruler, etc.	3. Removal or separation from previous commitments. People 'leaving all'.
4. Being wise, cautious. Remaining with the established religion of synagogue and temple.	4. Commitment, following Jesus, cross-bearing, the yoke. People actually going with Jesus as followers.
5. Acting on science or logic; based on questions and debate. 'The paralysis of analysis.'	5. Discernment, insight, seeing the point at which to act. Sometimes Jesus clarifies this.
6. Presence of customary happenings in normal society: • outcasts kept in their place • society maintained • broad-minded tolerance, with Law maintained as generally good for society • love those who love you, within existing relationships • society's unfortunates receive charity but not change • sick and ministered to, but not liberated • groups remain within customary social relationships	6. Presence of aspects or bits of the Kingdom, such as: • outcasts finding a home • society being turned upside down • straightening, moral heightening, a discipline of limitation and concentration • trust, reconciliation, filiality, mutual dependence, openness between persons, loving enemies • poor being given good news, prisoners being liberated • blind seeing, dead rising, broken being healed • sinners being forgiven, alienated being reconciled
7. The continuing cycle of things is maintained. People act in continuity with their pasts in expected ways	7. Sense of there being a *kairos* a 'right time'. People think and act in discontinuity with their pasts in unexpected ways
8. People continue acting on logic or reasonableness, as interpreted by accredited teachers	8. Discernment of hidden reality; unreasonableness; perception of truth by unexpected people
9. Everyone has good news. God loves everyone equally.	9. Good news for the poor. God's equal love for all means some are compensated.

It is interesting that this opposition between cultural insider and radical disciple continues in gospels which were written at a time when, if we may judge from other parts of the New Testament, both models were present in the earliest churches. Clearly, the gospel model of radical discipleship persists in the Christian tradition as a closer picture of an attitude and style which cannot anywhere be replicated *in toto* by anyone. What is important is that one gets as much of it as one can.

The same is true for radical discipleship in Christian history, and today. The genius is to discern which parts of it are relevant and possible at any particular time. The disciple does that.

Such, then, is the gospel picture of radical discipleship. Its political relevance stems from two sources. First, from the political activity of Jesus, to whom the disciple is discipled. Second, from a preparedness for some of the aspects of discipleship to be persisted with in political contexts.

JESUS AND POLITICS

1. Jesus' action was totally political, that is, it related to the whole life of human beings within all relationships in the actual conditions of the time. As a Jew, Jesus' whole life and teaching were practical, and this became part of the political situation. *Therefore*, Christianity is a germ, a seed, for change, within all political situations.
2. Jesus' action in relation to the religious situation was political, since the religious situation of Judaism was a system which determined everything in a person's behaviour. The religion was not just a part of life, it was the whole of life. So that everything Jesus did was a threat to Judaism as a total religio-socio-political system. *Therefore*, Christianity is a radical rejection of every attempt at a theocratic or totalitarian state.
3. Jesus was not a political leader, a revolutionary, or a leader of an uprising against Rome. As a Jew, he longed for liberation from the Roman rule. But the accusation that he 'incited people to revolt, opposed tribute to Caesar, and claimed to be a king' (Luke 23. 2) was false. More likely, the Jewish authorities feared him (John 11. 47–9) and delivered him up for 'envy' (Mark 15. 10). *Therefore* Christianity sits loose to nationalism, and constitutes a critique of all violent political revolt, while also opposing totalitarianism.
4. Jesus set up an alternative political reality in the disciple group, characterised by community of goods, abandonment of personal possessions and finance, and mutual dependence. It was this reality which continued as the early Church. *Therefore*, in this sense, Christianity is communistic. But communistic not as an imposed political system. Jesus heralds and inaugurates a voluntary communism.
5. Jesus sought to overcome the most vicious effects of the politico-religious bondage imposed by the systems of his day, by concentrating upon healing, transforming and liberating those at the bottom of society. Out of them, he declared a new kingdom-community which

was intended to rival all existing political, social groupings. *Therefore*, Christianity is a revolutionary force, by elevating the poor and marginalised into being the normative group in God's Kingdom.

6. Jesus proclaimed and exemplified the superior importance of the human person above all systems. All politics must be seen under God. Neither the Roman system (John 19. 11–34) nor Jewish ambitions (Matt. 24. 43–6) can be affirmed. Rather, he inaugurated an alternative community of equality, love of neighbours, poverty, humility, forgiveness and opposition to power and prestige. *Therefore*, Christianity is its own alternative, political reality, within all existing systems and alongside them.

7. Jesus renounced the use of power and violence. By calling the poor and the little ones to places of privilege (Matt. 25. 31–46, Luke 14. 21–4) he elevated the power of the powerless. He exercised and commanded love of enemies (Luke 6. 27). These radical reversals were to be carried out as disciplines within the disciple group. But they were intended ultimately as a policy for all. *Therefore*, Christianity is an alternative power system.

Such, then, are some of the political stances which stem from the one to whom a disciple is discipled. I turn, next, to pick up some of the distinctive aspects of radical discipleship in the Gospels, and then point to some of the policies which disciples today might adopt.

DISCIPLESHIP AND POLITICS

The radical discipleship tradition has a great deal to contribute to the discovery of relevant ways for Christians in the nineties. I use eight elements from Mark's Gospel, and conclude ways in which the elements constitute relevant political stances and bases for Christian action today.

1. *The Call*. Christian existence begins in a contrary consciousness, based on using the secular as model (fishing) for an alternative vocation (Mark 1. 16–20). *Therefore*, because of the oppression of our new, acquisitive, self-centred world view, Christianity must be discovered again as a contrary consciousness, in which renunciation, vocation and a call to be different are assumed.

2. *Common Life*. The twelve are called 'to be with him' (Mark 3. 14). Distinctive lifestyles, customs, disciplines and economic communism result from this new existence in community. *Therefore*, in a situation where political parties represent only varieties of the same model,

common-ism, economic sharing and common life need to be lived out as a visible alternative.

3. *Alternative Values.* The common life of 'giving up' issues not only in domestic difficulty (for Jesus, Mark 3. 31–2), but also in a new 'family' (Mark 3. 34–5), which carries with it its own economic, cultural and communal disadvantages and opportunities – as in the 'hundredfold' (Mark 10. 28–31). *Therefore,* reducing family loyalties, and possessing only economic self-interest alliances, Christians manifest values of sharing across cultural, economic and social divides.

4. *Seed of Societal Change.* The alternative existence, consciousness and social/cultural/economic arrangements of the disciple group are seen by Jesus as a 'seed' of change and reversals within society. Hence the images of salt (Mark 4. 49f), good soil bringing returns (Mark 4. 1–20), lamp (Mark 4. 21–3), growing seed (Mark 4. 26–9), and mustard seed (Mark 4. 30–2). *Therefore,* withdrawing to some extent from participation at every level in secular society, disciples get on with being 'seeds of change', 'centres of contrary consciousness', 'experimental stations for new arrangements'.

5. *Mission in Acted Parable.* The mission into the society to preach the kingdom (Mark 6. 12; 1. 15) is also a way of representing the cutting edge of the kingdom (Mark 6. 7–11). *Therefore,* in public communication and acted parable, disciples represent 'the cutting edge of the Kingdom', parabolically, symbolically, in dramatic form.

6. *Alternative Social Norms.* Alternative social norms, those of the Kingdom, are asserted over against those of existing religion and society – as in eating corn on the Sabbath (Mark 2. 23–8) and also over against those of existing power and politics – as in the entry into Jerusalem (Mark 11. 1–10). *Therefore,* training is needed for disciples in alternative social norms and behaviour.

7. *Taking On the Powers.* Especially in chapters 10–13 in Mark, the disciples learn from Jesus to oppose the existing religious and political powers. Jesus is a 'politician'. *Therefore,* distancing at times is needed from existing political options, so that powers can be identified, analysed and opposed.

8. *Setting up Alternative Powers.* The whole of Jesus' activity, while rejecting existing powers, is to set up alternatives. Jesus is a 'Counter-Politician'. *Therefore,* counter-politics becomes the new pedagogy, with disciples developing alternative powerbases which can both affect political issues directly, and also influence existing party political position.

Such, then, are some of the major orientation points for the Christian disciple, following the way of discipleship in the Gospels, and then seeking contemporary ways of acting in public and political life. It does not constitute programmes. But it certainly constitutes basic stances, and ways of acting, on the assumption that now as in gospel times, Jesus represents a new way of being human – and political – which has its implications for discipleship.

To these basic stances and ways of acting, the radical disciple also adds another strand – that of immediate identification between a particular gospel story or element with a particular contemporary issue or possibility. The disciple 'makes a snap' between the contemporary possibilities and those of gospel story.

Three examples of this are very common – and, I think, are justified and coherent with the total position. In each case, the disciple looks at a gospel element and identifies its presence in a contemporary possibility.

1. *Lifestyle*. Radical disciples look at the gospel description of 'happiness'. It is in Luke's Gospel, where all the 'beatitudes' are comments of Jesus not on people in general, but on the life of disciples. Jesus looking on his disciples said:

> Happy are you who are poor, for yours is the kingdom of God.
> Happy are you who are hungry now, for you will be filled.
> Happy are you who weep now, for you will laugh.
>
> (Luke 6. 10–22)

The contemporary disciples look at this, observe the rapacity, over-consumption and superficiality of the society around, and hear a call to an alternative lifestyle, one of radical modesty, going backwards, underconsumption, being less, reduction in ambition and presumption about what is needed for wholeness of life.

The beatitude proclaimed by Jesus is not, at least at this point, any comment on any so-called blessedness of the economically poor as such. Rather, it is a statement about those who became poor when they became disciples. So, today, the radical disciples see lifestyle changes as part of their discipleship, but also as significant responses in a divided world of rich and poor. An ecology of radical modesty is both a personal dynamic and a political witness in a world of over-consumption, expansionism, waste and 'development'.

2. *Sharing*. Radical disciples are drawn to the stories of sharing, community of goods, mutual dependence and economic interdependence. They take seriously the gospel stories of disciples leaving all and

following Jesus. They see many people today as like the 'rich young ruler', who rejects discipleship because of his possessions (Mark 10. 17–22). Obviously, the original forms of the sharing were the economic arrangements of a wandering charismatic disciple group. The disciples could say 'We have given up all'. Not unnaturally, Peter asks, 'What do we get?' The answer of Jesus is striking:

> There is no-one who has left house or brothers or sisters or mother or father or children or fields, for my sake and for the sake of the good news, who will not receive a hundredfold now in this age – houses, brothers and sisters, mothers and children, and fields with persecutions – and in the age to come eternal life. But many who are first will be last, and the last will be first.
>
> (Mark 10. 29–31).

From this, radical disciples look for alternative communitarian arrangements within their own company. Hence, today, as in most ages, the constant emergence of communities and movements, of Base Ecclesial Communities, and of cooperatives. The disciples thus set up 'mini-communities' which can be parabolic and exemplary both for fellow-Christians and also for society. An ecology of mutual support is commended in the body politic by this discipleship commitment, an ecology which demonstrates mutuality and interdependence and heralds a new wholeness in the world.

3. *Pouring Out*. Radical disciples, like all politicians, suffer from the temptation of believing that what they are doing out of their own commitments and convictions, actually is for the good of all. For disciples, the model for this is the disciples' Master. The Christ-persons, Jesus or disciples, have to pour themselves out, like power going out (Mark 5. 30), like precious ointment (Mark 14. 3), like flesh and blood (Mark 14. 22–24). A dramatic instance of this is the Johannine statement about the grain of wheat:

> Truly, I tell you, unless a grain of wheat falls into the earth and dies, it remains just a single grain; but if it dies, it bears much fruit. Those who love their life lose it, and those who hate their life in this world will keep it for eternal life. Whoever serves me must follow me, and where I am, there will my servant be also. Whoever serves me, the Father will honour.
>
> (John 12. 24–6)

'Serving me' means being a fellow servant with Jesus, and carrying on the dynamic of self-giving. 'Losing life' is not only the way to 'saving

life' (Mark 8. 35), it is also the way whereby a continuous and re-
peating pouring out of energy and power takes place for the good of
all society. A world in which all is brought to fullness – the many
grains – is constantly renewed by the voluntary self-giving of the
seed, rising as a new plant only because it has died as a seed. An
ecology of radical self-offering replaces technology, industry and
rapacity against nature or people, in favour of a wholeness of all
things renewed. Such a renewal is not achieved by enlightened
policy 'from the top', but only by the mystery of redeeming power
at the base or core, 'from the bottom'. The ecology of wholeness for
all hangs upon the willing dying of some, or some parts of all.

DISCIPLESHIP IN PRACTICE

Such are some of the ways in which, in our time, parts of the Christian
story are being rediscovered in the experience of radical disciples. That
constitutes both a problem and an opportunity for contemporary theology. What is the significance for Christianity that this is happening? I
believe we have to rewrite our theology, in Urban and Liberation terms,
because of new things like this happening.

But what is its significance for politics? Does it constitute an escap-
ism, a prophetic witness, or a political stratagem?

In every time of affluence or conformity, this Call to the Journey
Downwards emerges from the Gospel. In our time, it has taken hundreds
of people, many of them politically aware, into inner cities and housing
estates, into community houses and community activism.

The physical location of this new exodus in the inner city is, I believe,
significant. All the classic contemporary issues and dilemmas are writ
large in the inner city. For the locals, all the points at which public
policy is thought to succeed – education, technology, money, health, living
standards, lifestyle, success – are unsuccessful. If we want to see how
society's ideals have failed, the inner city is a good place to be.

Also, the inner city witnesses the pathetic and even laughable failure
of the middle-class entrepreneurial, technological, and ideological contributions. In north-east Sheffield, in the inner city and housing estate
areas in which I work, all the 'solutions' to the problems of the poor
have been tried and found wanting. Solutions in planning, health, social
services, inner city regeneration, unemployment schemes, housing action,
transport changes – all have achieved something, but have not basically

transformed society. They have even produced new problems. On top of these we now have the triple wonders of the derelict steelworks valley next door to us – Sheffield Development Corporation, 1991 Student Games, and the Meadowhall Shopping Centre!

All this means that the inner city is the place where you can really see what our society is about. It confronts us with the mirror image of our success society. Only by looking at the bottom of a society can you really see what is happening at the top.

Certainly, the inner city is not issuing any invitation to success-oriented businessmen and enlightened entrepreneurs to 'come over and help us'. Rather, the inner city represents so clear an alternative to the dominant mores, that the emigrés from the straight society discover there colleagues, teachers, and role models. And the inner city becomes the place where the former middle class becomes reduced to a common and basic humanity.

I believe that as an option for Christian attitudes in politics, this exodus into the inner city of the former slaves of the enterprise society is very significant. First, it overcomes the monochrome assumptions of culture-affirming Christianity by demonstrating a valid and visible alternative. Second, it contributes to the classic guilt of middle-class Christians by showing how at least some of them are called to be parables of self-sacrifice. Third, it revives the vital tradition of radical discipleship as a present option. Finally, it provides a place for the classic form of monastic community, Desert Fathers, Quaker village, Moravian settlement, etc., to find contemporary expression.

How significant politically is this latest Christian exodus into the desert? It is easy to ridicule it, alongside more 'responsible' attitudes. Yet, in my experience, it is done by people who are extremely 'responsible' in terms of politics. I would name a number of ways in which it has political value.

1. It confronts the assumptions of the present political status quo. It begins from a different place from the starting-points of contemporary political parties. It questions the dominant assumptions of the educated, enlightened, technological, meritocratic, upwardly mobile, individualistic policies of the present political parties.
2. It provides an independent place for experiments with new styles and responses, which do not require the whole society's compliance. A concentration on small projects becomes possible. Alliances of a street-level kind, independent of multinational corporations and the vagaries of the Stock Exchange are needed if the whole of society is to achieve any new developments and orientations.

3. It conceivably constitutes a prophetic foreshortening of the eco-logically simple lifestyle of all people in the future. It is one outpost, hopefully, of non-exploitative attitudes towards people, nature, and materials. The whole world cannot afford any longer the rape of the poor, the blacks, the women, the natural world, or even the human mind, by the oppression and the victimisation of the power-ful and moneyed. A new ecological lifestyle emerges only where these things are not possible any more.

4. It provides a place and style whereby some of the most pressing and insoluble of our problems can be worked with. The increasing number of the underclass in our society desperately need some human moves to alleviate their total isolation. The racism of our society needs to be worked with at the level where the races dwell side by side. The finance-dominated society, in turn, will not solve its own problems by endless modification and self-criticism. They may be solved by the contrary images and stories of human whole-ness and fulfilment existing outside of it.

Does it not represent a proper strategy for us?

We have assumed that we could have confidence in a consensus, and that we could win over the majority so that an acceptable, new consensus would emerge. But what if the consensus is likely to remain basically hostile to what we hope for, much less the Kingdom of God? Do we not need a strategy of the Long March, of getting on with the future, of partial advance, where advance is possible, of building up in secret what is needed ultimately, everywhere, openly? Is not our place actually nearer to that of the early disciples, small groups of alternative people within a great state which either ignored them or was hostile to them?

In terms of public life in general, the inner city is an easy place from which the consensus of modern Britain can be questioned. A new, liber-ated, pluralistic Britain of coherent but distinguishable ghettos may result. The consensus will never benefit the outsiders. Outsiders them-selves must generate some alternative models.

The hope of radical discipleship in politics is that the Christian story and movement might contribute some pioneers and labourers for an egalit-arian, non-exploitative, reconciled Britain. It is a bid for the future, based on some self-giving in the present. Like the movement of Jesus and the first disciples.

5 Religion and the Politics of the Environment
Hugh Montefiore

This lecture is concerned with religion and the politics of the environment. But it is not immediately apparent that religion ought to enter into this question at all. After all, God created the universe so that somewhere or other in the cosmos intelligent beings could evolve who would be capable of eternal communion with himself. In the words of the Westminster Confession, man's chief aim is to glorify God and to enjoy him for ever. Is not religion therefore concerned simply with God and the individual soul, rather than with politics of any kind, including the politics of the environment?

This question, upon further analysis, turns out not to be so simple as it at first appears. The human soul is incarnate within a human person, and human persons are not just individuals, they also have a corporate side to their personality. Since religion requires a response which is reflected in human behaviour, and since politics is about the way in which people regulate their corporate behaviour, it follows that religion, or at any rate the Christian religion, is bound to be concerned with politics. In fact there is a sixfold basis for Christians to attempt to influence the political process, which in this lecture I can do no more than mention in passing; firstly, because they need to stand with the poor who are also the proper concern of society; secondly, because they need to make ready the kingdoms of men for the coming of God's Kingdom; thirdly, because they have a duty to promote justice within the state; fourthly, because this is one of the ways in which they can practise loving their neighbours as themselves; fifthly, because living out the implications of the Incarnation means involvement in the world; and sixthly, because it is incumbent on them to see that natural law is honoured in society as a whole.[1]

However, it is one thing to justify the involvement of Christians in the political process: it is quite another to justify their involvement in the politics of the environment. Is not our present concern with cleaning up the environment just another example of the secular fallacy of progress? Would it not be better if religion kept instead to its job of cleaning up the human soul? Is not the doom and gloom with which environmentalists

oppress us really a secularized form of eschatology, which substitutes the
threatened demise of *homo sapiens* for the threat of the Last Day when
we shall all appear before the judgement seat of Christ? Are not Christians who are trying to improve the environment simply conforming to
the world's newest fashion, and climbing on to the latest secular band-
wagon? Yesterday it was the Health Service, and the day before that it
was Apartheid; but today it is the Environment.

These may sound like merely rhetorical questions; but nonetheless I
shall attempt to answer them. I have to say that I see no Gadarene rush by
church people to pursue environmental politics, or even to be concerned
with the environment at all. I speak as someone who first published on
this subject way back in 1966,[2] a quarter of a century ago, and who has
been trying in vain to get the Church as a whole interested in the environment ever since. Indeed, there are some secular environmentalists
who not only believe that the Church has been backward in its concern
for the environment, but also that it has actively promoted its spoliation.[3]

The environment needs to be cared for, not only so as to preserve its
usefulness for mankind, but also for its own sake. Indeed, right at the
very beginning of the Bible, the truth that all creation has intrinsic value
is declared with compelling power in the Creation story myth (where God
says: 'Behold it is very good'[4]). In the following chapter of Genesis
there is a second myth of Creation, where we are told that God placed
man in the garden to care for the natural world and to use it, not to abuse
it. It was only when man disobeyed the natural law of God that he found
that the environment had become hostile. It is interesting that in the
recent Government White Paper called *This Common Inheritance* we are
told that 'the starting point for this Government is the ethical imperative
of stewardship which must underlie all environmental policies'.[5] But the
concept of stewardship only makes sense if a steward is accountable to
someone. The White Paper is strangely silent on this score. 'We do not
hold the environment as a freehold, but only on a full repairing lease.'
Who, then, is the landlord? It can only be God. If God is the ground of
our concern, we have three interests to serve as we obey his commands.
First there are our own interests, because by poisoning our environment,
we can damage (and even destroy) one another; second, there is the interest of posterity, because by causing longterm pollution or by exhaust-
ing non-renewable resources without ensuring adequate alternatives, we
are depriving posterity of its heritage; and thirdly, there is the interest of
the environment itself, of which we are the stewards and trustees, and
which God saw was very good. In this last category we must include

not only the elimination of species, and the destruction of ecological balance, but also the destruction of important wildlife sites, such as the present threat that the Broads will become a wildlife desert.[6]

I hope, therefore, that we may agree that the Church does have a duty to be concerned about the environment. But is this duty not best discharged by persuading individuals to be environmentally friendly? Does not each one of us need to be vigilant in avoiding waste of precious non-renewable resources, and in guarding against pollution? Certainly that is true. Words are always easier than action. It is one thing to deplore global warming: it is quite another to restrict one's own central heating on that account, or to lay out capital on full insulation of one's home and on longlife light bulbs, even though in the end this will bring personal economies. It is one thing to deplore the amount of carbon dioxide emissions: it is quite another to restrict one's speed when driving, or voluntarily to use public transport where one's motor car would be far more convenient. No rules or regulations about the environment introduced by government are going to be effective without the goodwill of the population, and without a change of personal attitude on the part of most of us. The Greek word for that change of attitude is *metanoia*, commonly translated in the New Testament as repentance. Yes, religion is certainly concerned with changing the attitudes of individuals.

But not only with that. However powerful may be the appeal of religion (although we surely have to admit that its admonitions are hardly even heard by many people in Britain today), there will always be many who prefer their immediate advantage or convenience to the longer-term interests of their community. In fact, the consciences of many people today are becoming aroused by damage to the environment without their being able to give a reason for these feelings of moral outrage. Nonetheless, human nature is such that both curbs and disincentives are required to prevent further damage; and these are needed on a national scale. For all that can be done voluntarily by individuals and by firms and by professional organisations, the force of law is still required; and since the introduction of law is a matter for government, we find ourselves pitchforked into the politics of the environment. These laws can fall roughly into two categories. On the one hand, it is possible to use the forces of the market to regulate demand and supply in accordance with the national good. Various techniques can be used,[7] such as the costing of environmental damage, the use of environmental audits, project appraisal, the purchase of licenses to deal in scarce non-renewable resources, all under the general principle that the polluter pays. On the other hand, it is possible to issue rules and regulations binding upon all, which is a rather blunt-edged way of dealing with a situation, but sometimes the best.

It is not the job of the Church to attempt to pronounce on the best method of promoting environmental wellbeing. That belongs to the sphere of economics, not that of religion. Nor is it the job of the Church to research the facts of the situation: that is the sphere of scientists in research institutes, university laboratories and government organizations. Of course, it is always the duty of the Church spokesmen to ascertain the facts before they make any pronouncements; and in this area the facts and their proper interpretation are not always easy to discover. But that applies to everyone, not just to churchmen. Moreover future environmental effects are seldom cut and dried, and so what is usually required is action to be taken as a result of the informed assessment of future risks.

What is the proper sphere of the Church in the politics of the environment? It needs to assert first principles, and to clarify morality. It needs, when necessary, to bring pressure on governments to act for the common good rather than to condone bad practice and to acquiesce in *laissez faire*. There are many bad reasons for such acquiescence. Lethargy can overcome governments as much as it can individuals. Furthermore, no government likes to introduce measures which will be unpopular and may diminish its number of supporters, especially towards the end of its term of office. Measures for the environment may take some years to bear fruit, but governments, in this country at least, need never look ahead more than five years to a general election. Governments may not wish to spend money on environmental improvement when they have other financial preoccupations, and they may be unwilling to take measures which would involve increased taxes. Again, governments may be influenced by powerful lobbies, especially if these contribute heavily to party-political funds. At the same time it must be recognised that there can be good reasons as well as bad for *laissez faire* in situations which seem to call for immediate action. Environmental controls might cause severe unemployment in particular industries, or might put a country at a disadvantage in world trade, or could even restrict the availability of certain foodstuffs which at present almost all can afford.

Clearly measures of environmental control are more complex than might appear at first sight, intermeshing with economics, trade, industry and agriculture and even international relations. Nonetheless the Church, while it has no competence to decide environmental policies, does have a duty to press the high moral ground on behalf of posterity and the intrinsic value of creation.

It also lies within its proper sphere to point out any failure to reveal the facts to the public and even to mislead them. Perhaps I may give a couple of examples here of what I mean in the field of both energy and transport. I have no quarrel with the Government White Paper *Our Common Inheritance* as a whole: indeed there are excellent things to be found in it, including a first-class chapter on First Principles. But I did notice that, when discussing fossil fuels and alternative sources of energy, there is a certain reserve. It is not made clear so far as energy from nuclear fission is concerned, that global disenchantment with the Fast Breeder Reactor has destroyed the dream of unending world-wide electrification. As for nuclear fusion, we have as yet barely reached breakeven point in the laboratory so far as energy is concerned, with commercial application not yet on the horizon. Fossil fuels have limitations, although coal, the most plentiful of our reserves, deserves a mention. Coal is often decried nowadays. No doubt miners can be tricky people; but there is plenty of coal left. The reasons given against burning it is that it spreads sulphur pollution and causes carbon dioxide. But sulphur can be removed by scrubbers and if coal is burnt in liquid oxygen, the carbon can be removed in liquid or solid form, and carbon dioxide gas completely avoided. Why are we kept in ignorance of all this?

Nonetheless, if we want plentiful continuing supplies of energy, we have to look to renewables. It is the task of the Atomic Energy Authority at Harwell to research into these, with such meagre resources as are devoted to them. Inevitably a body primarily devoted to nuclear power would be unlikely to lay much emphasis on these alternative sources of energy. Whatever be the reason, the story of British windpower is a tragic one. Once we led the whole world in wind technology, but lack of resources has meant that research has faltered, and now we have to go overseas for up-to-date development. Wind machines can now produce energy more cheaply than by nuclear reactor; but no one could guess from the White Paper that, compared with some countries, we are far, far behind in installing them. Denmark for example is planning to produce 20 per cent of its total energy from wind, while ours is a mere trickle by comparison.

The story of wave power is not only tragic: it is actually scandalous. The Duck wave-power machine had its funds discontinued, the EC is still advised not to give money for its development despite the fact that there has been gross misinformation from the Department of Energy which has only recently been corrected. In fact costs for wave power are now

comparable with those for nuclear power, and while nuclear costs go up
as the scale of commercial output is increased, those of windpower and
wavepower reduce. Yet the White Paper gives no indication of all this,
and — another scandal — it does not even so much as mention wave
power in its account of renewables!

So far as transport is concerned, officialdom has cold-shouldered
public transport over the last ten years, and roads have been favoured
over railways (and incidentally the Royal Society for Nature Conser-
vation reported in 1990 that the present £12 billion road-building
programme threatens hundreds, and possibly thousands of important
wildlife sites, including many scheduled as of special scientific interest[8]).
Although official private car projections into the next century far exceed
any possible increased road capacity, there seems to be no attempt to
restrain private car use. What do we find in the White Paper about roads
and railways? In advising travellers how to help in reducing greenhouse
gas emissions and air pollution, the option of taking public transport
appears as only the sixth priority in a list of eight possibilities;[9] yet it is
one of the more important options open to the traveller.

This is not the only bias against public transport in the White Paper. A
diagram showing the comparative contributions of the various transport
modes to carbon dioxide levels fails to mention pedestrians and bi-
cyclists (whose contribution is nil); and, worse still, it makes out British
Rail's Network SouthEast to be almost as bad in this respect as motor
travel.[10] But the diagram is inaccurate (it does not take account of the
fact that Network SouthEast provides mostly peak services when gas- and
oil-fired generators produce less carbon dioxide than the coal-fired
ones in more general use). Worse still, it fails to point out that the comparatively high amount of carbon dioxide per passenger in buses and
on certain sectors of British Rail is due to existing low occupancy rates.
Buses are shown to produce per passenger as much as 50 per cent of
the carbon dioxide from a car; but the average occupancy rate of a bus
is taken as only 17. If government measures encouraged more people
to go on buses, closer to their 88 maximum, the carbon rate per passenger would be correspondingly lower. As for trains on the provincial
sector, the figure is calculated on an average occupancy of only 43 pas-
sengers per train, and the carbon dioxide rate is shown as almost as
bad as travel by car. Admittedly there is a note to the effect that the
carbon dioxide rate per passenger on this sector should be halved when
new rolling-stock arrives; but this note is in the smallest type in the
whole report, and I had to get a magnifying glass in order to read it! It
is misleading to show statistics of what is the case without explanation

and without showing what would be the case if more travel were to be diverted to public transport.

I mentioned that one country can be put at a commercial disadvantage by adopting more rigorous environmental controls over its agriculture and industry than other countries, and that this is one reason why the environment is now a matter for international politics. So far as Great Britain is concerned, many regulations come from the European Parliament, and this has in general been to the benefit of the environment, except in some cases, such as the density of hens in battery houses and percheries and free range flocks, where these regulations have led to a lowering of British standards.[11] Pollution often does not respect national boundaries. One has only to remember the effect of Chernobyl on Welsh sheepfarmers, not to mention acid rain in Scandinavia caused partly by our own factory chimney emissions. Again, the dumping of waste in the North Sea, or the fouling of the Mediterranean, not only affects the countries carrying out the dumping, but all who fish there. Furthermore, many species have vanished through human beings destroying the conditions under which they thrive. Many species are endangered and international regulations such as the one on whales are needed to conserve species and, in the case of fish, to safeguard future stocks of valuable food. Once again, this is a matter of international politics.

There is one most important factor which ought to be a matter for the international politics of the environment; but it has been found to be too sensitive a subject for international politics to deal with. I refer to the question of human population. This year there will be an additional 90 million people on the planet. The rise is exponential, as increasing numbers of people reproduce themselves. There are now over 5 billion people, there will shortly be 6 billion, and there could even be 8 billion within the lifetime of some in this cathedral tonight. The strain on natural resources is likely to become too great. Already firewood for fuel is under great pressure, millions die of starvation, and the annual increase in the world's harvests can no longer keep pace with the annual increase in world population. Obviously more people cannot live than there is food to keep them alive. But it is not only future mass starvation that is to be feared. There is the certainty of increasing desertification, environmental degradation and pollution and the elimination of more species, which will inevitably result from attempting to shelter, feed, clothe and in other ways satisfy more people than the planet can support. Here in Britain our population is at about replacement level. But in some other countries it is soaring. As Japan and China have shown, governments can and indeed should alter this, by disincentives and other means to prevent population increase; and here religion could play its part. UNICEF reports that in some Third World countries a priest not only holds marriage preparation classes but also instructs couples in basic hygiene. Alas, the largest Church in Christendom takes no such similar steps over the limitation of families. A quarter of a century ago, I called the papal ruling in *Humanae Vitae* as 'ecologically speaking the most disastrous utterance of the century' and I see no reason twenty-five years later to dissent from that judgement.

There is an even more compelling reason for the international politics of the environment. Dangers are appearing not only for individuals, nor merely for nations, but for the whole race of mankind. It is helpful here to consider what are the essentials for human life on earth. We require a reasonably consistent and equable climate. We need protection not only against radiological hazards on our planet, but also from harmful rays which come from without. We need a sufficiency of clean and unsalinated water. We require a soil sufficiently fertile to produce the food that we need. We require air to breathe, an atmosphere with roughly the same mix as that to which we are accustomed. Trace elements are necessary for our health, and we require an ecological equilibrium which permits their recycling. We also require unpolluted oceans, for they cover most of the earth's surface, and they perform certain functions which ecologically speaking are necessary for human wellbeing. Yet many of these essentials are now either under threat, or they are beginning to be threatened. There is room for some doubt about the situation, because the ecological interactions are often so complex that it is impossible to have adequate models to predict with certainty the future, the immediate or longer-term future. At the same time action is needed long before a critical state is reached, because by then the position may have become permanently irreversible. We are beginning to reach an unprecedented epoch in the history of our planet, when the actions of human beings are threatening its vital systems. Clearly the resolution of this threat demands international cooperation. It is a question of the politics of the environment. Fortunately, it seems as though this is beginning to be more widely recognized. The recent Montreal Protocol, agreeing to phase out CFCs, and the Second World Climate Conference at Geneva in the autumn of 1990, are certainly signs of hope for the future.

These are complex matters. For example, ICI, the largest producer of ozone-destroying chemicals in Europe, has produced as a substitute to the CFCs which is destroying our ozone layer another gas which is 5750 times as effective as carbon dioxide when viewed as a gas which produces global warming![12] We may find ourselves with a remedy which is worse than the fault.

Global warming itself can be caused by many factors, such as a reduction in the albedo, the white surface of the planet which reflects back heat into space: this would be reduced if the polar ice were to melt. Global warming, however, is now being aggravated, mostly by the so-called greenhouse effect, when gases are produced on earth which permit the sun's rays to warm the earth, but which prevent the heat from escaping into space. These gases are of different kinds. They include nitrous oxides, which come from farming and burning fossil fuels; methane, which comes from rice paddies, from rotting vegetation and the digestive tracts of cattle; CFCs used for refrigeration but now being reduced and phased out; and most of all carbon dioxide, which comes from the burning of wood and fossil fuels.

Carbon dioxide is buffered in the oceans, and it is converted by the action of chlorophyll in green plants both into the oxygen which we breathe and into the carbon which forms the basis of the planet's life systems. The developed world produces the worst carbon dioxide pollution – the USA, for example, with 5 per cent of the world's population consumes 25 per cent of the world's energy. But deforestation, causing a serious reduction in carbon dioxide conversion, takes place mostly in the Third World. In the international politics of the environment it is essential to gain the cooperation of all, Third World, Russia, China and the developed world. But the Third World complains that its development would become impossible if it had to pay the expenses involved in environmental protection, while it is now suffering environmentally from damage caused mostly by the developed world. In any case, most of the income of the Third World has to go on servicing debts to the developed world, and the recent increase in the cost of oil has made the plight of its inhabitants even more desperate. They badly need such cash crops as logging provides. Obviously assistance from the developed world is required if these countries, often with burgeoning populations, can both emerge from their dire poverty and at the same time play their part in the world's fight against environmental dangers, of which global warming is only one example. In the same way, the countries of eastern Europe and Russia find themselves with terrible problems, with a run-down economy and appalling environmental pollution.

The need to reduce carbon dioxide emissions poses very difficult problems for *all* countries, developed and undeveloped. Increased energy efficiency can make an enormous difference, as became apparent when oil prices soared when OPEC first began to operate some years ago. But unless we get unlimited energy from the fusion process – and there is no sign at present that this can be done – there will have to be tremendous changes in attitudes, not least over the unrestricted use of the private motor car: what Mrs Thatcher has called approvingly 'the great car economy'. Pollution from motor vehicles accounts for some 20 per cent of carbon dioxide emissions in this country. The cost of reducing by 2005 our emissions back to the present 1990 level, will not be great, but it scarcely scratches the surface of the problem. Even if every nation stabilised its carbon dioxide emissions overnight, the amount in the atmosphere, already 25 per cent above the pre-industrial level, would continue to rise indefinitely, bringing ecocatastrophe to the planet. International agreement is urgently required. Major differences exist between governments over targets and over financing. The UN will have to decide in 1991 whether to prepare a treaty on global warming gases to be agreed at the United Nations conference on the Environment in Brazil in 1992. Since supplies of energy are required for the production of almost all goods, it may well be that, if we are to keep our climate under control, we may even have to restrict world wide the world's manufacturing capacity, and so peg our material standard of living. This may sound to some the grossest heresy; but the truth is that the planet cannot for ever sustain industrial development.

Is it possible that there can be a sufficient global change of attitude and sufficient world cooperation to enable this to happen? Can the nations of the world find the will to control their environment in the light of the global situation that is now beginning to develop as a result of overpopulation, pollution and the approaching exhaustion of non-renewable resources? While recent world conferences do give some cause for some hope, I do not myself think that the fundamental change of attitude on the part of literally billions of people which is going to be needed can possibly take place without religious motivation. Governments cannot introduce environmental measures without the good will of their electorate: indeed, recent history strongly suggests that they will not even consider such measures unless forced to do so by the will of their electorate. But what will motivate people to demand changes which involve not just one country, but international cooperation throughout the world? People in Third World countries are desperate to raise their standard of living: people in the developed world are sustained by a materialist culture which demands ever-increasing wealth. Human beings can be moved by fear in the short term; but the perils of which I am speaking are not short-term visible dangers. There is no power on earth so strong as that of religious motivation. I mean the conviction that we are stewards of the planet, trustees for posterity, priests of the created order pledged to 'represent' the interests of animals, plants and all organic matter, accountable before God for the way in which we discharge our duties in these respects.

If that is the commission that is laid upon the Church, how is the Church discharging that commission? What has it done to change the attitudes of individuals, to clarify the moral issues in the national politics of the environment, and to use its world-wide influence on international politics? I have to admit that it has done little in the past, and seems to plan to do little in the future.

The Church of England first raised the question of the environment in a symposium of essays published in 1966, and edited by Edwin Barker, then Secretary of its Board for Social Responsibility.[13] The Board published in 1972 an introductory report on the subject called *Man in his Living Environment*. When I became Chairman of the Board, I persuaded the Board to set up an Environmental Reference Panel of experts, and in 1986 there was published *Our Responsibility for our Living Environment*. However, neither of the debates which followed these reports matched the urgency of our situation. In 1975 a group of theologians, set up by Dr Ramsey, Archbishop of Canterbury, in connection with the Doctrine Commission, produced *Man and Nature*.[14] This was a report on the theology of the environment rather than a programme for practical action. At present the Board for Social Responsibility is engaged in producing a statement of Christian stewardship towards all creation. The British Council of Churches has taken one initiative in this field, commissioning in 1977 a series of public hearings on nuclear policies concerning the building of commercial fast breeder reactors.[15] And that is all that has happened in Britain. The Dutch Reformed Church has taken initiatives in Holland, but very little has been done by national Churches as a whole.

The Roman Catholic Church, by far the largest church worldwide, has neglected or avoided environmental questions in its series of great Encyclicals. The Orthodox Churches, which have the best theological record on the subject, are not in the habit of involving themselves in practical affairs. The successive Lambeth Conferences of the Anglican Communion have usually contained a reference to the environment among the many resolutions passed, but these have received little publicity and have not led to action by constituent Churches.

The World Council of Churches has a better record. In 1973 it staged a large conference at the Massachusetts Institute of Technology on 'Faith Science and the Future' in which these matters were addressed. A few years later it held a series of public hearings in Sigtuna in Sweden on nuclear energy, chaired by our own Archbishop, Dr Habgood. In 1990 the World Council held in Seoul, South Korea, a worldwide convocation on Justice, Peace and the Integrity of Creation. There were some sensible resolutions on the environment, among others on social justice and the establishment of peace. But few people take much notice of the World Council resolutions. It has a tendency to politicise the Gospel, and to involve itself in particular matters of strategy in which it has no expertise (approving, for example, of a fossil fuel tax[16]). No compelling demand for Christians worldwide to concern themselves with the environment, including national and international politics, emerged from the Seoul Convocation. Roman Catholics were angry that their hierarchy did not permit them to join in fully. It seems that the Churches cannot even formally cooperate in trying to save the planet!

Perhaps there is no one single ecclesiastical body that can stimulate the Christian motivation that will be needed to help save human beings from damaging our environment irreparably. In any case more than Christian motivation is required. The cooperation of all the mainstream religions is needed. Stewardship of nature is part of the Judaeo-Christian inheritance. Muslims understand man as *kalifah*, or deputy, for God. Buddhists, with their belief in reincarnation, believe that all life is to be treated with respect, a view shared by most forms of Hinduism. Despite very different religious convictions, there is still an important area here for practical cooperation; and the combined pressure of the mainstream religions would have a considerable impact on worldwide environmental politics.

The Worldwide Fund for Nature, in conjunction with ICOREC (the International Consultancy for Religion, Education and Culture) has taken some useful initiatives here. Its President, the Duke of Edinburgh, was reported recently to have visited the Pope, to try to modify his/Church's views on contraception, and so help to reduce world population. In the past this organisation has assisted in launching Creation Festivals and Festivals of Faith and the Environment in several Anglican Cathedrals,[17] and also in producing literature for schools. The Worldwide Fund has been also concerned with other faiths. To mark its 25th Anniversary Celebrations, it enlisted the Pope and invited to Assisi religious leaders from Buddhist, Christian, Hindu, Jewish and Muslim faiths, where important Declarations on Man and Nature were made.[18] This was the first time that religious leaders from these five great faiths had met together in a spirit of goodwill and cooperation in the face of the environmental threat to mankind. Perhaps this important kind of initiative is best left to a world-wide non-religious organization. Advances made by one particular faith might seem to adherents of other faiths as a form of presumptuousness. Future initiatives like that in Assisi are urgently needed.

I hope that enough has been said to emphasise the urgency of the threat to our environment, and the need not only for Christians to involve themselves in environmental matters, but also for religious bodies to motivate people to engage in the national and international politics of the environment. The need is urgent. Little is being done; but the opportunities are great, and the effects of religious pressure to change attitudes could be enormous, and indeed decisive.

NOTES

1. For an exposition of these six grounds, cf. H. Montefiore, *Christianity and History* (London, 1990), pp. 17–32.
2. 'Man's Dominion' in *The Responsible Church*, ed. E. Barker (London, 1966).
3. Cf. M. Nicholson, *The Environmental Revolution* (London, 1970), pp. 264 ff. The most quoted essay was Lynn White's 'On the historical roots of our ecological crisis', *Science*, vol. 155 (10 March 1967), pp. 1203–7; but more recently he has blunted the edge of his argument, merely claiming that Latin Christianity 'provided a set of presuppositions remarkably favourable to technological thrust' ('Continuing the Conversation' in *Western Man and Environmental Ethics*, ed. I. G. Barbour (Reading, Mass., 1973) p. 58.
4. Genesis 1. 31.
5. *Our Common Inheritance*, Cmnd 1200 (London, 1990), 1. 14.
6. Cf. an unpublished internal report of the Nature Conservancy Council reported in *The Observer*, 2 September 1990.
7. Cf. D. Pearce, A. Markandya, E. Barbier, *Blueprint for Survival* (London, 1989).
8. *Head-on Collision* (London Wildlife Trust, 1990).
9. *Our Common Inheritance*, p. 268.
10. Ibid. p. 73.
11. Cf. R. Harrison *Farm Animal Welfare – what progress if any?* (Hume Memorial Lecture), UFAW, 1987.
12. Cf. *New Scientist*, 7 July 1990, p. 16.
13. H. Montefiore, 'Man's Dominion' in *The Responsible Church* ed. E. Barker (London, 1966).
14. *Man and Nature* ed. H. Montefiore (London, 1975).
15. The transcript of proceedings was published as *Nuclear Crisis: a Question of Breeding*, ed. H. Montefiore and D. Gosling (London, 1977).
16. *Now Is The Time* (WCC, 1990), p. 31.
17. Winchester (1987), Coventry (1988), Canterbury (1989), Salisbury and Washington, DC (1990).
18. *The Assisi Declarations* (WWFN, 29 September 1986).

6 The Prophetic Tradition and Human Rights –
An essay on religion and politics
Julia Neuberger

It is an enormous honour to be asked to speak here tonight, in Canterbury Cathedral, chaired by an academic for whose work I have the highest respect and about whom I have written an uncharacteristically rave review. But the subject is far from easy. Obviously, I have come to speak out of the Jewish tradition, and more specifically out of that nonorthodox section of Judaism that rejoices in the name of Progressive, or Liberal, whose founding fathers and mother (there was only one mother – in British Liberal Judaism the founders were entitled the three Ms, and I innocently thought, coming from the other bit of Progressive Judaism in Britain, the Reform movement, that this was a reference to a group of companies. But the Ms stand for Mattuck, Montefiore and Montagu, the last of whom, the Hon. Lily Montagu, was indeed female, and formidable at that.) These founding parents of Liberal Judaism felt that they spoke out of the prophetic tradition within the Hebrew Bible and Judaism. The leader in this respect was the most scholarly of the three, Claude Montefiore, who wrote a mass of papers and essays and books on the subject of prophetic Judaism, of Liberal Judaism, and of the relationship between Judaism and Christianity. It is he who summarized the role of the prophets and saw them as the key to the ethical teachings of Judaism:

'Rich and poor meet together . . .' Well, it is true to say that there are few areas of London where you can now walk freely without being asked for money by beggars, usually – but not always – young, usually – but not always – homeless, and sometimes with young children in tow. If you walk down to Waterloo, and into the underpasses, or cross Hungerford Bridge on foot from the Embankment to the Festival Hall, or walk up from the Strand into Covent Garden, it will be a constant, polite request: 'Can you spare some change?' Or they will not even ask, but sit there, eyes unfocused, with a notice on a piece of grey cardboard: 'Homeless. Please help'.

If you walk round the back of the Strand Palace Hotel, or round Temple Gardens, by Temple tube station, where the fat-cat lawyers operate by day, at night, in every doorway, in every ventilation outlet, you will find a curled-up person sleeping in a cardboard box, ragged perhaps, if older and part of street life, but much more likely not to be, but to be part of that huge group, an estimated 20 000 – 50 000 people, the figures are unclear, who sleep rough in London every night.

Rich and poor together. . . . Homelessness, and particularly young homelessness, in Britain, has many causes. Those causes are political – the selling-off of public housing stock, without replacing it, or not encouraging a dependency culture and therefore forcing young people to move on. But they are also far more profound than just political. And they reflect a malaise about which the prophets had much to say:

> Woe to them that devise iniquity,
> Who design evil upon their beds.
> When morning dawns, they execute it,
> because they have the power
> They covet fields and they seize them,
> Houses and take them away,
> They defraud men of their homes
> and people of their land.
>
> (Micah 2: 1–2)

Or take Isaiah's cry on the same subject:

> He looked for justice,
> But behold violence!
> For equity
> But behold iniquity!
> Woe to those who join house to house
> and add field to field
> till there is no room
> and you must live alone in the midst of the land.
>
> (Isaiah 5: 7–8)

In Canterbury Cathedral, home to the just-departed Archbishop, Robert Runcie, who so bravely in his report on Faith in the City, his Commission's analysis of what was – and is – happening in our inner cities, it is appropriate to reflect on the extent to which the Church of England has, from time to time, also looked at the prophetic tradition and used it in order to be fearless in criticizing both political stances and, more profoundly, the underlying social attitudes that made such human misery and degradation possible.

We Jews have been less brave – for a variety of reasons. One is considerable disagreement in our midst as to what, as a Jewish tradition, we have to say. The Chief Rabbi's views on the inner city are very different from those of many other Jews – and certainly from mine – and his view as to what a Jewish response to these issues might be is utterly different from what we might hear from many Jewish MPs or Jewish lawyers or many progressive, and, indeed, orthodox, rabbis.

But what we have lacked is courage, failing to recognize the prophetic tradition's insistence on values of justice and compassion, and equality, for all human beings. Jews have been brave and effective in campaigning for our fellow Jews, in the Soviet Union, for instance. We are excellent at campaigning when we believe ourselves to be under attack – as, for instance, in getting Jim Allen's play, *Perdition*, removed from performance at the Royal Court Theatre, which may in itself have a worrying implication when one thinks about the right to free speech.

Yet I believe that Judaism, based on the prophetic tradition, with its strong *this*-life affirming thought pattern, seeing this world, this life, as the stage on which God's plan for humanity and man's own route to salvation will he played out, prophetic Judaism with its message of justice and compassion, still has a clear view to give about these matters – a view of society and community which may accord with those of other groups, but which has a unique strength. And progressive Judaism, particularly those sections within it which regard themselves as being within the prophetic tradition, the great tradition of the Hebrew prophets who cried aloud about injustice and who tore into the rich and oppressive elements within their societies: 'who sell the poor for silver and the needy for a pair of shoes . . . ' (Amos 8. 6), particularly has a message for wider society, in Britain and worldwide, which we have been slow to address.

There are, of course, reasons why we have been so slow. One is the effect on the Jewish community, of Europe particularly, of the Holocaust – the sense that we have only been able to look inwards, tend to our wounds, come to terms with what has happened, what took place – rather than look out and beyond ourselves. It led to our dealing more or less effectively with social issues in our own midst, but denied us a voice in the wider world, denied us – a denial of our own making – the ability to express that prophetic tradition we have inherited, adding to it the practical and legal remedies that the rabbinic tradition taught us to construct.

But though there are many Holocaust survivors left amongst us, as well as their children, themselves not wholly unaffected, the European Jewish community has to combine its memories, its message of *zachor*, 'remember', with a look outwards and beyond itself, into the wider communities in which it lives, and recognize the message of that prophetic tradition on which its philosophy is largely based, and accept the paramount importance of justice and equity within the prophetic, and the Jewish, thought-pattern.

And for the purpose of recognizing rights-based traditions in Judaism, it is essential to look both at the prophets of the Hebrew Bible and at the Exodus story. For the Exodus story has a universalistic message as well as its particularistic one, especially as interpreted by some modern *haggadot*, the service books used for the Passover service and meal in Jewish homes each year at the *seder*, on the first (and sometimes second) nights of Passover: 'We too give thanks for Israel's liberation; we too remember what it means to be a slave. And so we pray for all who are still fettered, still denied their human rights. Let all God's children sit at this table, drink the wine of deliverance, eat the bread of freedom.' (Union of Liberal and Progressive Synagogues, 1981)

That has to be set alongside prophetic injunctions that festivals are valueless if at the same time the poor are oppressed, enslaved or in chains: 'Your countless sacrifices, what are they to me? says the Lord. . . . The offer of your gifts is useless . . . New moons and Sabbath and assemblies I cannot endure. There is blood on your hands. . . . Cease to do evil and learn to do right, pursue justice and champion the oppressed, give the orphan his rights and plead the widow's cause.' (Isaiah 1: 11–17)

The concept of justice, interpreted to some extent as charity, social justice, is interwined with that crucial journey from slavery to freedom. In one sense, the journey is taken entirely literally, but it also became spiritualised, symbolic, a justification for observing the ten commandments – 'Remember you were slaves in the land of Egypt' – and particularly the Sabbath, when everyone has a right to rest from labour, Jew, non-Jew, slave, free person, man, woman, or animal. And if a slave said he did not want to leave his master after a six-year stint, the ceremony through which he had to go was to have his ear bored through with an awl. The implication that one must cherish freedom is not difficult to find!

Freedom and social justice, as in the giving of charity, are the mainstays of early Jewish thought about human rights. The obligation is to give 10 per cent of one's income, which implies a process of evening up injustices in a far from ideal world. Haim Cohn, former Israeli Attorney General, makes the excellent point that the duty to give *tsedakah*, this 10 per cent social justice payment, implies a collateral right on the part of the poor to receive it. (H. Cohn, *Human Rights in Jewish Law*, Ktav, 1984, *passim*). Within the Hebrew Bible and the rabbinic literature, the principles on which human rights thought is based are emphasized again and again. The supreme dignity of humanity, which is essential for a concept of human rights, is enshrined in early biblical texts. Creation itself is in 'the image of God'. All races are included, by tracing descent from Adam and then Noah. But the bulk of the law covers such areas as slavery, sabbath observance, the rights of those pursued in blood-feuds for cities of refuge and the duty to establish fair courts of law.

This is combined with an emphasis on the giving of charity, and on particular ways of giving, especially doing it in such a way as to liberate the poor person from ever needing to ask again. The great Jewish teacher Maimonides (1135–1204) listed that as the highest of his eight orders of charity, starting at giving willingly, but not enough, to giving grudgingly, to giving to an unknown recipient, and so on until the highest of them all. All this is well attested long before the concept of human rights ever existed. That was arguably the invention of the Puritan leveller tradition and John Locke, but it has had a profound influence on modern Jewish thought, particularly in the United States, with its Declaration of Independence which traces rights back to the divine: 'All men are created equal, that they are endowed by their creator with certain unalienable rights, that among these are Life, Liberty, and the pursuit of happiness.' This is, in itself, a peculiar statement, as Judge Pollak observed: 'By tracing these rights to the creator and by characterising them as unalienable, the Declaration gave important impetus to the principle – which also had its antecedents in Locke's writings – that some individual rights exist in perpetuity apart from and above the laws periodically prescribed by particular kings and legislatures vested transiently with the power to govern.' (L. H. Pollak, *The Constitution and the Supreme Court*, 1968, vol. 1, p. 18) Its roots lie in the Biblical loathing of unnatural death, of which each one must be accounted for to God. Until that account is made, and until the explanation is accepted, the killing and those unnatural deaths are a blemish on the land, and the land itself will 'vomit up' those who perform great acts of violence. The prophets speak out against this senseless, mindless killing: 'I said, Listen, you rulers of Jacob, you chiefs of the house of Israel. You, who ought to know what is just, who hate the good and love evil, who tear the skin off the people and the flesh from their bones, who eat the flesh of My people, and flay the skin off them and break their bones . . .' (Micah 3: 1–3) But the roots of the American Declaration may also lie elsewhere, not usually adduced as a source, the prophetic, and particularly

Isaianic, insistence on the nature of the human mission: '. . . I the Lord
have called thee in righteousness, and have taken hold of thy hand, and
have kept thee and set thee for a covenant of the people, for a light to
the nations: to open the blind eyes, to bring out the prisoners from the
dungeon, and them that sit in darkness out of the prison-house. I am
the Lord, that is my name.' (Isaiah 42: 6–8)

But what is the reason for this duty to open the blind eyes and rescue
the prisoners? It is in the nature of a religious duty, a *mitzvah*, a positive
commandment. These are rules to live by. And the converse of these
duties to perform certain acts on belief of others, as Haim Cohn has
pointed out, is their right to have that act done for them. Therefore, the
duty to perform a certain duty, such as this general one of pursuing freedom on behalf of others, or the more particular ones of the giving of
charity, imply a collateral right on the part of the recipient of these acts
to receive the benefits of the efforts of others.

Similarly, the emphasis on fair trials and a proper judicial system appears first in the prophetic writings as a general injunction, particularly
in Isaiah's description of the ideal ruler in chapter 11: 'He will judge the
poor with equity and decide justly for the lowly in the land.' (v. 4) It
then appears as more detailed law later on, if one assumes a later composition of the Pentateuch, in the laws of Leviticus 19 and 24: 'Ye shall
have one manner of law.' (Lev. 24. 22), and Numbers: 'One law and
one manner of law shall be for you and the stranger that sojourneth
amongst you' (Num: 15: 16). This is further elaborated in Deuteronomy,
with the magnificent injunction, based on the equality precepts so
emphasized by the eighth century prophets, that: 'Hear the causes between your brethren, and judge righteously between every man and his
brother, and the stranger that is with him. Ye shall not respect persons
in judgment but ye shall hear the small as well as the great; ye shall
not be afraid of the face of any man.' (Deut: 1: 16–17) Deuteronomy is
in fact a setting for the principle of the fundamental human right of
equality before the law. David Daube, in his essay on the rabbis and
Philo on Human Rights (in: D. Sidorsky: *Essays on Human Rights*) suggests that judicial procedure and equality before the law with its roots
in the prophets of Israel and its development in biblical and rabbinic law
are the first signs of what we would genuinely understand as rights-
based thinking in Jewish thought.

But although it is difficult to ascribe particular fundamental human
rights, as we have later codified them, to prophetic thought, it is undoubtedly the case that the general principles of fairness and equity, of
rights to shelter, food and clothing such as the UN Covenants guarantee

so ineffectively, are in fact there in the prophetic thought about how
human beings should treat one another:

'Cease to do evil, learn to do well, seek justice, relieve the oppressed,
judge the fatherless, and plead the widow's cause:' (Isaiah: 1: 16–17)
Indeed, one could argue, as Heschel did (A. J. Heschel: *The Prophets*,
New York, 1962, p. 201), that there was no distinction, or dichotomy,
between justice and kindness in the thinking at all. He quoted Niebuhr
(R. Niebuhr: *Pious and Secular America*, New York, 1958) as saying, in
terms that may be instantly recognizable to those of you who know well
the wording of *Faith in the City*: 'Justice was not equal justice but a bias
in favour of the poor. Justice always leaned towards mercy for the
widows and the orphans.'

Unspoken though it may have been, that thought-process became a
key part of Jewish thinking in the period of the Emancipation, for as
the USA became a haven for Jews and other minorities the doctrine
spread, and as Jewish emancipation occurred in eighteenth to nineteenth
century Europe, there tended to follow a view amongst Jews that it was
to their advantage to campaign for civil rights for themselves and others.
This was done both by attacking slurs upon themselves and by stressing
the universalism of institutions such as universities. The history of the
founding of University College, London, largely by Jews and nonconformists, because other universities were closed to them, is a case in point.

For in 1783 Moses Mendelssohn had argued in *Jerusalem* that the
State needed to be liberated from the Church, and Heine wrote not much
later: 'What is the great assignment of our times? It is the emancipation
not only of the people of Ireland, of the Greeks, the Jews of Frankfurt,
the blacks of West India, and similarly deprived peoples, but the whole
world, especially Europe . . .'

The Jewish endeavour had become inextricably caught up in the mainstream social and political liberalisation of nineteenth century Europe.
To some extent it was probably founded in self-interest, but it was also
theologically and morally founded in Judaism. Man is accountable both
for his deeds and his destiny, this world is the main scene of individual
human endeavour, and human life is paramount.

Therefore, within the law-based system, there came to be a duty to do
things for others which resulted in their having an implied collateral
right to receive, be it the gleanings of the harvest or protection from
oppression. That, in its turn, led to a fair judicial system, to due process,
and equality before the law. This was true of Judaism as a whole, but it
became the clarion call of early Reform Judaism with its prophetic fore-
bears, and of the Liberal, Universalist tradition.

Those are standard principles in the modern world, but in Europe Jews have a special relationship, perhaps, with the European Convention on Human Rights because it was drafted and ratified in the wake of the Second World War and the decimation of the Jews of Europe, as well as the destruction of other groups such as gypsies and homosexuals. Its historical significance is obvious, but its principles draw out much of what already exists in Jewish thought, basic principles of justice and value of freedom. That is a convention we should undoubtedly incorporate in British law, given that Sir David Maxwell-Fyfe, later Lord Chancellor Kilmuir, played such a leading role in its design in the immediate post-war period and that the UK was the first State to ratify it in 1951 (see A. Lester: *Fundamental Rights: The United Kingdom Isolated*, in: *Public Law*, Spring, 1984, pp. 46–72). Jews and others, such as Christians and Muslims who share that same tradition, who see themselves as within the prophetic tradition with its insistence on these fundamental principles of liberty, equity and justice should be pressing hard for incorporation, but as yet it is relatively few religious organisations who have lent their names to the campaigns to get the European Convention incorporated, and those that have are largely nonconformists in both the Jewish and Christian traditions.

It is interesting to observe that reluctance, for we all use the phrase 'human rights' too frequently. We use it to defend those we like against those we do not like – we Jews talk about the fundamental human rights of Soviet citizens, Jews especially, when we are loath to address the fundamental human rights of Palestinians, particularly those on the West Bank and in Gaza. We talk about fundamental human rights of black South Africans, but we are less eager to talk about the fundamental human rights of blacks in UK prisons, more likely to be there, and for longer, than white British citizens convicted of the same crimes. We campaign for Soviet Jews to be allowed into the US, but fail to campaign for refugees to be allowed into Britain, or for immigration controls to be relaxed for certain categories of people wanting to settle here.

And so, paramount to my mind, is the establishing of basic minimum standards of human rights, a lowest common denominator if you like, which across the political and religious spectrum from right to left can be recognized as the best we can do at any given time – which is legally binding upon the nations. I believe that human rights strand to be very strong as part of the justice theme of prophetic Judaism. And yet I also believe that we have been slow to recognize it. Each Passover, we Jews take part in that journey from slavery to freedom the Israelites took from Egypt to the Promised land. It is the memory of that journey which is

adduced time and again in biblical texts to justify the duty of the Israelites to perform certain acts of charity and social justice for particular
categories in society. 'For you know the heart of the stranger . . . for you
were strangers in the land of Egypt . . .' It is not only the story which
justifies remembering certain groups in society, but also the story
which underpins the recognition of fundamental human rights within
Jewish thought.

There is, of course, a further question as to what extent it is within the
prophetic tradition to campaign for changes in the law. Is the concentration on justice and equity in the prophetic tradition sufficient to force
us to campaign to achieve greater justice and equity within, say, the
British legal system? Should we agree with Samuel Horsley, Bishop of
St Asaph's in the last century, who said in the House of Lords: 'What
have the people of England to do with the laws except obey them?'
Should we not also campaign for their change and encourage the use
of law for educational purposes, with human rights legislation being
only a small part of a much larger task that lies ahead of us, though
crucial to it? For with its constantly re-emphazised duty to correct
oppression and to support the poor, Jewish teaching, particularly that
of the prophets, makes clear both the required action and the basic
underlying principles. And the very urgency of the tone of the prophets
is what, to my mind, is one of the key factors in suggesting that in-
herent within the prophetic tradition is the desire to change the status
quo, to act as reformers.

There is a strong message in the prophets to which we progressive
Jews, alongside many Christians and Muslims, describe ourselves as the
heirs. Yet we hesitate to put our noses over the parapet in case we are
attacked for holding the wrong political views – or merely, in our case,
for being Jews. With our tradition of respect for social justice and for
fundamental human rights, that will not do. If British Jews look to our
fellow-Jews in the USA, we see a plurality of responses to rights-based
issues such as we have not yet begun in Britain. They are more secure,
and happier in their diversity. We have failed in the UK to produce a
Jewish liberation theology such as Marc Ellis has written in the USA –
but the European Jewish experience, of all Jewish experiences, should
have led us to it. And though individual Jews have been key figures in
the race field for generations now, the community involvement is weak.
Yet Jews, like most Muslims in Britain, are partially protected by the
race relations legislation on the often somewhat dubious basis of ethnicity,
and many of us have experienced racism. With our tradition, and our
history, we ought to be at the forefront of campaigning on race issues.

The Prophetic Tradition and Human Rights

With the Jewish experience of oppression and a folk-memory of a journey from slavery to freedom, we, like Christians and Muslims, have a responsibility expounded in biblical law: '*Lo tuchal lehitallem*' 'You cannot hide yourself . . .' (Deut. 22: 3), and emphasized by the prophets. It is our responsibility to take on the task of the prophets, to open the blind eyes and to free the captive from his chains. And that's just the beginning of a process of recognizing the human rights tradition within the prophets of Israel, reaching towards an aspiration that seems far away:

> The Lord will make in this land
> For all nations
> A feast of rich foods,
> A feast of choice wines,
> Rich foods seasoned with marrow,
> Choice wines fully clarified.
> And in this land He will destroy the shroud
> That covers the faces of all peoples,
> The covering that is spread over all the nations.
> He will destroy death forever.
> The Lord, my God, will wipe the tears away from all faces
> And will put an end to the reproach of people over all the earth.
> For the Lord has spoken.
>
> (Isaiah 25. 6–8)

...tion Theology
...olitics
...owland

I recall three conversations I had on my first visit to Latin America in 1983. When I was in Mexico City I met Jose Portfirio Miranda, author of *Marx and the Bible* and an exponent of the theology of liberation whose writing had secured him a wide audience in Europe and North America. I was treated to a very gloomy set of predictions about the future of the theology of liberation: 'all that will be left of it in a few years' time will be our books', he said. It has to be said that he was speaking in a country where the theology of liberation has never gained a firm foothold and as a result the distinctive features of its theological and pastoral method are not much in evidence. The second conversation echoed some of these fears. I was at a celebration of one of the few 'middle class' Basic Christian Communities in São Paulo. During it one of the theological advisers of the group, who taught at the pontifical seminary, spoke of her fears about the crackdown on the theology of liberation which would precede the celebrations of the evangelisation of the Americas in 1992. She pinned her fears then on Lopez Trujillo of the Latin American Conference of Bishops and talked of the desire to present 'a pure church', unsullied by politics, to the Pope in time for the next conference at Santo Domingo in 1992. That meant, she suggested, breaking the power of the then progressive Brazilian Bishops' Conference. The third conversation was in contrast with both of these. In it Clodovis Boff, brother of the more famous Leonardo, himself a member of a religious community, spoke of the Basic Ecclesial Communities (the CEBs) as a force in Brazilian life which could not be stopped. He said that whatever the attempts by forces of reaction to put a stop to the process of change and renewal in the Church leading to involvement in action for social change there could be no putting the clock back. Or as he more graphically put it, 'once the toothpaste has been squeezed from the tube there can be no putting it back in again'.

I mention these conversations at the beginning of this lecture because, seven years later, there are elements of truth in what all three said. Over recent years in many countries of Latin America, particularly Brazil, there has been a spate of appointments at episcopal level which has seen the progressive bishops replaced with conservatives or moved to peripheral dioceses. This has meant a clear shift in the balance of power in the powerful Brazilian Bishops' Conference away from the progressive and often controversial style of recent years. Observers in Brazil suggest that the Church is everywhere on the retreat back to altar and presbytery. Yet despite all that, at the grassroots the Church as the people of God is as involved as ever. Millions of ordinary men and women whose names will never make the theological libraries of Europe and North America are struggling in the midst of hardship and injustice. They are convinced that their faith emboldens and enables them to engage in activity which confronts the powerful and struggles for better conditions for themselves and the poor here and now. They may have less recognition from official ecclesiastical organs but the extent of their faith and their commitment cannot be in doubt. The next few years promise to be tougher for them. Some will become disillusioned. But many will carry on, confident that their faith in Jesus demands it of them. Are they misguided, the dupes of the widely discredited secular theologies of the sixties or have they in fact got insights into the nature of the gospel which we do well to learn from and take to our hearts? My concern in this lecture will be to explore something of that interpretation of Christianity and suggest reasons why it is not only a valid reading of the Christian tradition but one which has grasped a central insight which we ignore at our peril.

The theology of liberation has taken different forms throughout the world. In all of its manifestations, however, there are two basic features. First of all, God is to be understood in the experience of oppression and poverty as a God who identifies with those who experience injustice. Secondly, no theology can be done without an account about that experience of God as well as attention to the language of theology built up over the centuries. Even though the best-known example of the theology of liberation is from Latin America, many related types of theology have emerged from various parts of the Third World. The extent of their convergence may be gauged by the proceedings of the Ecumenical Association of Third World Theologians (EATWOT). My knowledge is such that I cannot begin to do justice to the various characteristics of Minjung, Black, and feminist theologies. What I shall do in this lecture is concentrate on Latin American theology of liberation. My main focus will be on Brazil, partly because it is the form I have seen at first hand and partly because in terms of importance, theologically and institutionally, Brazil can legitimately be considered the crucible of the Church's experience of the theology of liberation.

THE BASIC ECCLESIAL COMMUNITIES (CEBs)

Throughout Brazil tens of thousands of small groups meet regularly in *favelas* or rural villages for worship, Bible study and reflection on the everyday realities of poverty and injustice which confront them. For thousands of ordinary Brazilians the dialogue between the reality of poverty and the hope and inspiration offered by the scriptures has engendered a commitment to social change at local and national level based on popular participation and insight. These small groups, known as Basic (because they are rooted in the lives of ordinary people and communities) Ecclesial Communities, are a significant component of the contemporary political as well as ecclesiastical scene. They are made up and run by lay people. There is little suggestion of edicts being passed down from on high, though, equally, there is a recognition that priests and religious have a legitimate contribution to make to the development of understandings of contemporary discipleship. It has until recently been difficult to drive a wedge between the so-called 'popular church' and the mainstream catholicism in Brazil. Certainly there are tensions, particularly in those dioceses where there is less sympathy towards the CEBs. But Brazilian Catholicism is characterised by a widespread acceptance of the CEBs and their central role in being the Church in contemporary Brazil, a fact which is evident from the episcopal support of the CEBs' assembly in 1986 and equally evident in the most recent conference in Caxias in 1989.

The CEBs have over the years enabled the pursuit of a variety of different interests from many groups: trade unions, the political parties, the neighbourhood groups, the landless movement (where they have taken important initiatives in land reform over the years), the slum-dwellers, marginalised women, of fishers, of the aged, of the physically handicapped, of children, of blacks, of the Indian nations. Its concerns include women's participation in church life; the cause of the oppressed; commitments to political parties 'so that they can bring these parties the liberating ferment of the gospel', and land reform. The land is a pressing issue in contemporary Brazilian politics. Hundreds of thousands of peasants have found themselves ejected from land they have farmed for generations in the interests of the growing agro-business, so important is this for economic growth and the servicing of the foreign debt. Even if land reform legislation were enacted, the problem for many poor people is how to obtain redress from the courts without adequate legal support. Fine sounding words and phrases in state legislation is no substitute for the ability to implement that legislation on the ground. In the latter particularly we may glimpse something of the controversial activities in which CEBs have been engaged. They pursue the struggle for land reform, participating peacefully in actions such as resisting land expulsions, occupying unused land, communally organising occupied lands, pressuring government agencies, accompanying landless workers, and encouraging the Church to set an example of land reform.

There is a growing concern for the rights of indigenous peoples, particularly on the occasion of the celebration of 500 years of evangelisation in Latin America. The memory of the victims of colonisation should be recovered, be they Indian, blacks or other oppressed peoples, to allow for, as they put it, 'a new and courageous liberating evangelisation of the whole continent'. The problem of the indigenous people is particularly sensitive. Nowhere is the tension between justice for the possessors of land and the economic needs of contemporary Brazil so starkly put as here. They were the first to experience eviction from their land when it was despoiled by the Spanish and Portuguese conquests. The concept of liberation itself in its more obvious Old Testament guise of the liberation or deliverance of the people of God from oppression and their journey to a promised land is a potent story. It relates directly to the experience of the people, particularly when many of them have engaged in their own exodus and wanderings seeking better things in Brazil in waves of emigration from the poor north-east to the big cities of the south.

The growth of internal immigration within Brazil, particularly from the impoverished north-east, to cities like São Paulo during the period of the so-called economic boom in the late sixties and early seventies and more recently from the south to Amazonia caused severe social dislocation. The conditions facing those uprooted from rural Brazil were awful. Drawn by the promise of a better life as the economy expanded, those who were desperately trying to keep body and soul together drifted to the big cities, particularly in the prosperous south-east of the country. Those who arrived at the bus station with only those possessions they could bring with them resorted to making makeshift homes on any piece of spare land available or under motorway arches. It was this desperation which led to the mushrooming shanty-towns (*favelas*). Even in the *favelas* rents are extortionate. Those who do occupy land and build their rudimentary dwellings are harassed. Private security firms are hired by land speculators to evict even those who have gained title to the land; those who are squatting are harassed by police which provokes violence, and deaths are all too frequent an occurrence in some areas. Recourse to the courts is often difficult. Even with the return to democracy in Brazil the plight of the homeless in cities like São Paulo con-

tinues to deteriorate. Now immigration from the countryside has slowed
down, even though the plight of millions in the countryside has not
improved. During the time of the economic boom there was work: men
could participate as labourers in building projects, luxury homes for the
urban élite, for example, while the women could get work as maids for
that same group. In a time of economic recession work is not so plentiful, but that has made women's work essential for existence. In situations where it is not possible for friends and relatives to look after
children, thousands of children are left to join hundred of thousands more
children in Brazil's cities to roam the streets and increase the already
alarming problem of 'the street children'. Estimates are difficult but
some have suggested that as many as twenty million children are left
in various forms of abandonment. There is a problem of cataclysmic
proportions for Brazil when one considers that three-fifths of Brazil's
population is under the age of twenty-five.

   Close links were forged between the Churches and other groups
struggling for human rights during the dictatorship of the late sixties and
seventies. The Church was instrumental in setting up commissions on
human rights and later the CEBs have played a prominent part in the left
of centre Workers Party (PT). The development of popular movements
covers a wide range of positions and the CEBs offer one expression
of it. Grassroots participation during the period of the military dictatorship (1964–85) was focused on church-based bodies which provided an
umbrella for individuals from different backgrounds to meet and work
for common goals. It was perhaps that experience above all which laid
the foundations for the fruitful dialogue and cooperation between the
Churches and various groups struggling for justice for the majority. The
common interest in this goal, the shared experience of persecution led
Christians and politicians and trade unionists on the left to sink their
differences in search of a more humane environment for ordinary people
to live in. Throughout the period of the military dictatorship the Church,
particularly in cities like São Paulo, was tireless in defence of human
rights, and Christian people themselves suffered torture and even death.
This led to a long official campaign of vilification of leaders and basic
communities as crypto-communist.

   In the last decade or so, pastoral programmes have been consolidated
with programmes of development in education, health and human rights
in which the political dimension of Christian mission is very much to
the fore, evident in a variety of educational projects. The consequence of
all this is that the activity of the Church is often focused on the CEBs.
In them the capacity of the people to unite and promote justice and

human rights has probably had a not insignificant role to play within the gradual return of Brazil to a more democratic form of government. Still there are pressing problems stemming from the appalling economic conditions in the country. Economic conditions there have deteriorated markedly in the last year since the election of the Collar government. Meanwhile there is evidence that the Church has retreated from the advanced political positions that it held in the seventies and early eighties. This is in part because of the greater freedom for political activity in the restored democracy but also in part because of the greater reluctance of a more conservative church hierarchy to be involved in more controversial kinds of political activity. Despite this, there is widespread support among grassroots Christians for the Workers' Party and its charismatic leader, Lula, who came so close to winning the presidential elections in Brazil last year on a platform of justice for the poor and the repudiation of the foreign debt.

The CEBs offer a space for hope in a situation which seems devoid of it. Also, they offer an opportunity for a different perspective on the reality of life. How often have I heard men and women saying that through their involvement in the CEBs 'their eyes were opened' to injustice and the possibility that things might be different. Confidence is gained for the powerless to act and have a sense of their own worth. Being involved in the CEBs leads to involvement in rural unions and grassroots political activity. Members of the CEBs do not wait for structural change globally or in society but start making changes at the grassroots, attempting to construct new ways of living together which they hope to see implemented in society as a whole.

The influence of priests and religious touched by European political theology has rubbed off on these groups, particularly in those dioceses where there has been a well-organised pastoral programme. But it is not just a matter of the influence of a modern political theology. The understanding of evangelisation rooted in the Second Vatican Council, 'the bringing of good news into all strata of humanity and making it new' has had its part to play in the understanding of mission in today's world. Sometimes the ethos of the CEBs can be narrowly religious. Pentecostalism has its attractions in Latin America and is a rapidly-growing social force in the sub-continent. This has sometimes led to a loss of support from the Basic Christian Communities to pentecostalist and other protestant groups with grassroots involvement (though some of the members have chosen to exercise their political involvement through the trade unions and the PT). The rapidly-growing influence of pentecostalism and its appeal because of its apparently 'supernatural' character is a matter

which is disturbing leaders of the Church as also are the steady inroads
made by US-backed fundamentalist Christian groups with their allegedly
'apolitical' stance. Such developments are a reminder that the story of
Christianity in contemporary Latin America is incomplete without reference to the surge of support for fundamentalist groups, often supported
from North America.

EXPLAINING LIBERATION THEOLOGY

While liberation theology takes its start from the experience of exploita-
tion and poverty which is the lot of the vast majority of the population
of Latin America, the approaches to the Christian tradition manifest in
the writings of its various exponents cannot easily be reduced to a single
system. Of course, there are recurrent patterns which can be discerned in
much liberation theology (stemming from the option for the poor taken by
the Latin American bishops at their conference at Medellin), and some of
these common elements we shall examine in a moment. But liberation
theology is being carried out in many different situations varying from
war-torn countries like El Salvador and dictatorships like Chile via
emerging democracies of Brazil and Uruguay to the post-revolutionary
situation of Nicaragua. Thus, there are important distinctions to be
made between the various theologians of liberation.

   Liberation theology can be briefly described as a form of contextual
theology, in which the experience and circumstances of the interpreters
are given a prime importance as the first step in seeking to be a disciple
of Jesus. Thus there is no blueprint from the tradition, the theologians
or, for that matter, from the bishops which is going to offer unam-
biguous guidance independent of the circumstances in which the people
of God find themselves, struggling for justice amidst oppression and
want. A theological assumption undergirding this approach is that Christ
is be found there as well as in the tradition and the community of the
faithful gathered for worship. Action for justice in the face of a reality
of oppression is the prime step in theology. The poignant words of
the Son of Man in the story of the Last Judgement in Matt. 25. 31ff
provide a clue to the first step of this theology: Inasmuch as you have
done it to one of the least of these you have done it to me'.

   We may understand something of what this may mean if we look at
the outline of the liberation theology perspective sketched by Gustavo
Gutierrez, the founding father of liberation theology.

Gustavo Gutierrez has contrasted the approach of the theology of liberation with some of the concerns of European and North American theology in the following way:

> The question in Latin America will not be how to speak of God in a world come of age, but rather how to proclaim God as father in a world that is inhumane. What can it mean to tell a non-person that he or she is God's child? These were questions asked after their own fashion by Bartolome de las Casas and so many others in their encounters with native Americans. The discovery of the 'Other', the exploited one, led them to reflect on the demands of faith in an altogether different way from the approach taken by those on the side of dominators. (*The Power of the Poor in History*, p. 60)

The emphasis on the prior commitment which is the result of identification and action with and on behalf of the poor is a distinctive mark of the theology of liberation. Theology is not the articulation of a set of ideas worked out in isolation from the pressing realities which confront millions in Latin America. Rather theology emerges from the experience, the reflection on and action to change that reality of oppression and injustice which is the daily lot of millions. The discovery of truth is something found on the journey of life (a metaphor which is very popular in liberation theology). Liberation theology marks a different theological method. The way one will ascertain the voice of God is by starting where people are, because it is where poor and particularly oppressed people are that one will find God. It is with those people that the Bible is particularly concerned: the dispossessed, the widow, the orphan, the stranger, the prostitute, and the tax-collector. As Charles Elliott has put it, 'the liberation theologian will say very simply "the test for truth is the effect it has on people's lives. Is this proposition . . . actually liberating people or enslaving them?"' (Heslington Lecture, 1985).

At the heart of the theology of liberation is the belief that in the experience of oppression, poverty, hunger and death God is speaking to all people today and that God's presence among the millions unknown, unloved by humanity but blessed in the eyes of God is confirmed by the witness of the Christian tradition, particularly the scriptures themselves. It is this conviction, nurtured by the thousands of Basic Ecclesial Communities, which is the dynamic behind liberation theology, which would not exist in any meaningful sense without it and the preferential option for the poor. It is, as Derek Winter has remarked, 'theological reflection that rises at sundown, after the heat of the day when Christians have dirtied their hands and their reputations in the struggle of the poor for justice, for land, for bread, for very survival'. The understanding of theology as a secondary task, namely, one of critical reflection on life and practice, is not new to Christian theology. That subtle dialectic between the 'text' of life, viewed in the light of recognition and non-acceptance of unjust social arrangements and the other 'text' of scripture and tradition is the kernel of a lively theological, or for that matter any, interpretative enterprise. The world of the poor as well as their imagination provides shafts of light which can often throw into the sharpest possible relief the poverty of much First World interpretation.

It is a theology which places the victims of violence, injustice and oppression at the centre because the cross of Christ stands at the centre. Of course, the cross has always been at the centre of Christian theology. In liberation theology the cross stands as a challenge to the wisdom of the world which claims rationality and justice while leaving millions impoverished. The dying Jesus is not a reason for fatalistic acceptance of one's lot but a reason for living, struggling and if necessary dying for the justice of God and a glimpse of the good news in the everyday lives of the poor. Jesus is a martyr for the gospel. Leonardo Boff speaks of him thus:

> Jesus did not go unsuspectingly to his death. He courageously took on that risk; in his final period he hid himself from the Temple police, but he made no concessions to the danger of his situation; he remained radically faithful to his message. . . . He did not avoid his adversaries . . . but resolutely took the road for Jerusalem (Lk. 9. 51) for the final confrontation . . . [Jesus' martyrdom] was the result of the rejection of his message and person by those who refused to be converted to the kingdom of God. If Jesus was to be faithful to himself and to his mission, he had to accept persecution and martyrdom . . . The martyr defends not his life, but his cause . . . and he defends this cause by dying. . . . The resurrection of the martyr Jesus Christ has . . . this theological significance: who loses his life in this way receives it in fullness. (Boff, 'Martyrdom Today', *Concilium*, vol. 163, pp. 12ff.)

Mention of the story of Jesus brings us to biblical interpretation. The Bible is being used as part of the reflection by the poor on their circumstances as they seek to work out appropriate forms of response and action. There is often a direct identification of the poor with biblical characters and their circumstances, with little concern for the interpretative niceties which are invoked in applying the text to our own circumstances. In their use of scripture the resources of the text are used from their perspective of poverty and oppression, and a variety of mean-

ings are conjured up in a way reminiscent of early Christian and ancient
Jewish interpretation. The situation of the people of God reflected in
many of its pages are their situation. That aspect is well-brought out
by Carlos Mesters:

> the emphasis is not placed on the text's meaning in itself but rather on
> the meaning the text has for the people reading it. . . . the common
> people are putting the Bible in its proper place, the place where
> God intended it to be. They are putting it in second place. Life takes
> first place! In so doing, the people are showing us the enormous im-
> portance of the Bible, and at the same time, its relative value – relative
> to life. (Mesters, 'The Use of the Bible in Christian Communities of the
> Common People', in N. Gottwald (ed.), *The Bible and Liberation* (New
> York, 1983), pp. 132ff.)

In its rootedness in the Basic Ecclesial Communities (the CEBs) an
agenda is being set for the interpretative enterprise which is firmly based
in the struggles of millions for recognition and justice. The text becomes
a catalyst in the exploration of pressing contemporary issues relevant
to the community; it offers a language, so that the voice of the voiceless
may be heard. There is an immediacy in the way in which the text is
used because resonances are found with the experience set out in the
stories of biblical characters which seem remote from the world of
affluent Europe and North America. The Bible offers a typology which
can be identified with and at the same time a means by which the present
difficulties can be shown to be surmountable in the life of faith and community commitment. To enable the poor to read the Bible has involved
a programme of education of the contents of the biblical material so
that it can be a resource for thousands who are illiterate. In such programmes full recognition is taken of the value of the primary text, experience of life. Therefore, the poor are shown that they have riches in
plenty to equip them for interpretation. This is balanced with the basic
need to communicate solid information about the stories within the Bible,
of which many remain ignorant.

Most exponents of liberation theology would not want to claim that
they have the key to the proper reading of scripture (though there *are* some
who think the perspective of the poor is the criterion for a true reading
of scripture). The evangelical and popular roots of liberation theology
need to be recognised. It is known in this country as a result of the
translations which have been made of many of the writings of the leading liberation theologians from Latin America. The form which that
theology takes is normally not unfamiliar to the sophisticated theological
readership of the First World. That should not surprise us as most have

experienced the theological formation of Europe or North America. Nevertheless it is a facade which needs to be pierced in order to understand more clearly what precisely energises these writers. In a very important sense they have broken with that tradition in the perspective from which they have chosen to do their theology.

Those involved in liberation theology stress the importance of the wisdom and insight of the poor as the focal point of theology (something also noted by the Latin American bishops at their conference at Puebla). Both gain insights from listening to the poor reading and using scripture in the whole process of development and social change. The theologians find that this process of listening and learning has given a stimulus to their theology. This grassroots biblical interpretation provides a basis for the more sophisticated theological edifices they wish to build. Yet it is clear that the different experiences and worldview of the poor offer an unusually direct connection with the biblical text, which, whatever its shortcomings, has reminded Christians that there is another form of Christian reflection in which the insight of the apparently less sophisticated can inform the sophistication of the wise. The words of Jesus encapsulate the point:

> I thank you Father, lord of heaven and earth, for hiding these things from the learned and wise, and revealing them to the simple.
>
> (Luke 10. 21 REB)

The memory of the poor and outcast is frequently lost for ever from our view. Its retrieval is often the task of the sympathetic voices of another culture or class. Luke falls into this category. After all, Luke preserves the memory of a Jesus who represents an option which contrasts with that of the class of people he may be writing for. It is a mark of Christian historiography and theology from Luke onwards that there is greater concern to placate the mighty than to represent the cry of the oppressed. The shape of the story would be different if we sought to write it consistently from the perspective of the poor and voiceless. As the history of liberation theology itself indicates, the presentation of the 'voice of the voiceless' is almost inevitably in an idiom which is at once both more familiar and at a significant remove from the story that the poor might tell. There is a mediation involved in this which is inevitable and necessary. Like Luke's mediation of the story of Jesus, however, it can never fully capture the authentic voice of the cry of the oppressed and the reality of the liberation they hope to experience.

The perspective of the poor and the marginalised offers another story, an alternative to that told by the wielders of economic power whose story becomes the 'normal' account. The story of Latin America is a story of conquest. It is *Latin* America, a continent whose story begins only with the arrival of the Europeans. Liberation theology has its contribution to make to these projects. Of course, its complicity as part of the ideology imposed on the indigenous peoples of the sub-continent as the European conquerors swept previous cultures aside puts Christianity, in however progressive a form, in a rather difficult position. Yet its encouragement of the study of popular religion, whether Christian, Indian or Afro-American, must be part of its project to enable the story of the 'little people' of the sub-continent. In addition, it has championed the recovery of the religion of those with the Christian tradition who resisted the practice of conquest and despoliation, like Bartolome de las Casas and Antonio Valdivieso, whose ministry takes its part alongside those whom the conquerors would prefer to forget. The familiar story of the wars of kings and princes which all too easily becomes the staple fare of a normal view of life is challenged as the horizons are expanded by attention to the voices drowned out by the noise of the mighty. It is part of the task suggested in Walter Benjamin's words, 'In every era the attempt must be made anew to wrest tradition away from a conformism that is about to overpower it'.

A question remains. Is the theology of liberation merely a passing phase in the history of Christian doctrine, to join that long list of contextual attempts to make Christianity relevant?

A mere appeal to the emotions is unlikely to convince those who think that Christianity has little to say about change in this world save to hang on for the next. Indeed, there have been several questions raised about its propriety as a Christian theology from within the Roman Catholic Church itself, particularly in the First Vatican Instruction published in 1984. Many of the assumptions of that document were convincingly answered by various exponents of the theology of liberation themselves, and it was significant that a much softer line has emerged on the theology of liberation in general since (even though individual exponents have continued to be under a cloud).

Doubts may be raised whether Christian tradition sanctions a privileged epistemological stance for the poor. Clearly the Bible excludes the identification with the rich and powerful as being that of the perspective of God. Even if we might not want to identify the perspective of God solely with the perspective of the poor, we must accept that some balance is needed in the ways in which we view the world and the continuous exclusion of the perspective of the poor from our decision-making and our values cannot be tolerated. It is not just a matter of equality of per-

spective but also of seeking to do justice to the thrust of the Christian
tradition's perspective which in the words of a recent papal encyclical:

> the option or love of preference for the poor . . . is one . . . to which
> the whole tradition of the Church bears witness. It affects the life of
> each Christian inasmuch as he or she seeks to imitate the life of
> Christ, but it applies equally to our social responsibilities and hence
> to our manner of living, and to the logical decisions to be made con-
> cerning the ownership and use of goods . . . [this] cannot but embrace
> the immense multitudes of the hungry, the needy, the homeless, those
> without medical care, and above all, those without hope of a better
> future. It is impossible not to take account of the existence of these
> realities. To ignore them would mean becoming like the 'rich man'
> who pretended not to know the beggar Lazarus lying at his gate
> (*Sollicitudo Rei Socialis* p. 85)

That view may command wide support. Where the theology of liberation has parted company from conventional Christian wisdom is in its
argument that charity is not enough. That point was put with characteristic acuteness by Dom Helder Camara, former Archbishop of Recife
and Olinda when he said: 'If I give food to the poor, they call me saint;
if I ask why the poor have no food they call me a communist'. It is a
mark of the theology of liberation that it has not been ready to accept
things as they are as the moral and social order ordained by God.

If the theology of liberation had contented itself merely with discussion of the reasons for poverty, it might legitimately be criticized as a
theological talking-shop for the progressive wing of the Churches. But, in
addition to asking why things are as they are, it has sought means of
putting them right by demanding that the structures of society should
be changed in conformity with the reign of God. Throughout Latin
America there are numerous examples of small-scale activities in which
the poor are being empowered to challenge the inevitability of their
poverty and work for something which contributes to their dignity. So
it is not a matter of theological rhetoric only, but of the exploration of
realistic possibilities to enable the promotion of human dignity rooted in
the inspiration of the scriptures and sustained by the fellowship of the
people of God. My contact with Christian Aid over the last decade has
enabled me to see the way in which the values of the theology of liberation have formed small-scale projects which have empowered the poor
and been a practical demonstration of humanity and hope.

The theological assumptions upon which the theology of liberation and
the social action of the CEBs are based have been widely contested. It is

said that changing the world into the pattern of the kingdom of God is a human activity; that the kingdom can be built and can in some sense be realizable in this world; and that it is part of the task of evangelisation to bring about societal as well as human change. There is in my view a long and honourable pedigree for these assumptions rooted in the story the Church tells of Jesus of Nazareth. Indeed, it is no coincidence that the theologians of liberation are frequently to be found going back to this story as the foundation of their task. We have in the gospels not the story of charitable action or even of the wise teacher. Rather it is a life of activity rooted in the conviction that the reign of God when sorrow and sighing would flee away was not some pious hope but a present possibility. In this the powers of evil which afflicted individuals and society were being overthrown. The consummate challenge to the structures of the day came when, for whatever reason, Jesus set his face to go up to Jerusalem and met the powers that ran the political system of his nation.

The confrontation cost him his life, but in it we see the seeds of the conflict/struggle with the powers which was to find its theological expression in the *Christus Victor* doctrine of the atonement. The resurrection of Jesus is both a sign that things need not remain always so and a demonstration of the rectitude of Jesus' message and a pledge of the transformation still awaited. Christian faith means identification with that hope and empowerment with the life of a God who makes *all* things new. It is a mark of Christianity's tenuous links with its Jewish past that it has so often lost its grip on the realm of history as the arena of God's saving purposes, so that it can despise the material character of Jewish hope by juxtaposing it with its own, supposedly superior, spiritual salvation. In so doing, we not only diminish Judaism but also the character of salvation as set out in the biblical documents which are the foundation of faith.

To the charge that they have sold out to atheistic communism, many liberation theologians would echo the words of the Peruvian bishop at the meeting of Latin American bishops at Puebla. When conservatives accused liberation theologians of being Marxists thinly disguised as Christians he responded: 'Let him who is without ideology cast the first stone'. It is precisely that challenge which is at the heart of its most pungent challenges to theology. Liberation theologians question the use made of certain doctrines and ask in whose interests they have been utilised: for those with power in society or the poor? It becomes important, therefore, to challenge the dominance of the the the theological agenda set by First World theology when the pressing concerns of the poor in the Third World demand very different priorities.

The situation of Latin America and the poor in our world will not go away. In a recent article the Latin America writer Carlos Fuentes has written:

> Latin America . . . now faces the obligation to promote and defend social justice in a continent where the absolute number of poor people is continuously growing while income distribution becomes daily less equitable. It is a continent where wages decrease, jobs disappear, food becomes scarce, public services deteriorate, crime and insecurity grow, repressive bodies become autonomous in the name of the anti-drug campaign, malnutrition and infant mortality increase . . . (*Guardian*, 27 December 1990).

Confronted with the reality of the world's poor can Christians, too, remain silent? Even if we decide that the theology of liberation is an appropriate response to injustice at a particular time and a particular place which are different from our own, as part of the *oikoumene*, may we ignore the plight of other peoples because they are not our own? Are they not after all 'our poor' (to use Leonardo Boff's words) whose poverty and situation is in many ways the result of our own prosperity and well-being?

Any theology we do, any evangelisation we embark upon in this country cannot ignore the plight of our sisters and brothers in the so-called Third World, whether it be death squads in El Salvador, the brutal treatment of children in Guatemala so recently seen on our TV screens, or the terrible plight of the street children of Brazil banished from our television screens two weeks ago to be replaced by further analysis of the Gulf War. All Christians can understand the solidarity with the poor and oppressed. Indeed, it is part of our understanding of what discipleship is to do exactly that.

Something of that was well appreciated by Paul when he commended the 'collection' for the poor in Jerusalem. What is remarkable is the evidence of Paul's persistent concern to engage the relatively well-to-do members of his churches in an enterprise to deal with need. Whatever the motivation for this activity Paul clearly sees it as a significant contribution to the service of God, using language in Cor. 2. 9, which he uses elsewhere for this apostolic ministry in Col. 1. 24. It was a relief operation with few parallels in the contemporary world. That need is dealt with not in terms of the dependence of the needy on those who have plenty but by means of stressing mutual responsibility and the sharing of resources. It is very easy to get into a way of thinking that we can do something for the poor and share our material resources. But we can be recipients of their wealth of insight. Their struggles for justice and re-

cognition put them in touch with truths so easily drowned by our stam-
pede for material wealth: a sense of community, care of the earth, the
worship of a God who is concerned for the whole of life, not merely
the salvation of souls.

There is a legitimate question about the appropriate means of enabling
the poor to have a better life. There is a clear concern on the part of
those avid exponents of the North American spirit like Michael Novak
that the poor of the world deserve our concern. He is convinced that
the application of the American ideal to the situation of the poor will
bring about their betterment (as it has, he would argue, in South-East
Asia). Fuentes speaks for many of the theologians of liberation when
he questions whether the economic experiments of the last twenty years
have really benefited the poor (as he notes in the article already referred to):

> We are told that unfettered development of private industry will bring
> us prosperity, as it did in Germany, France or the US. All this . . . is
> to forget that the US is experiencing the worst financial crisis of the
> century [with] millions living below the poverty line in the land of
> conspicuous consumption of superfluous goods . . . All this so under-
> values the experience of 200 years of Latin American existence. . . .
> Since 1820 we have been subjected to the will of private industry
> both internally and externally, and our problems have not been solved.

The challenge that Fuentes says is posed for humanity is that of 'the Other'
(a word used by Gutierrez in the passage quoted earlier). . . That challenge
is one that Christians can recognise, for it is at the heart of the story they
tell: strangers, pilgrims, peripheral people, those who, in the words of
the letter to the Hebrews, are 'the deprived, oppressed and ill-treated . . .
of whom the world was not worthy' (Heb. 11. 37f). We 'see in the poor
the suffering features of Christ himself' (Pope John Paul II).

The theology of liberation may not always get right the balance between evangelical commitment and political action. But it surely is seeking to be true to the story which the Church exists to proclaim in word
and deed, in identification with the poor and outcast. There is in the
articulation of an appropriate response to their struggle for justice an
understanding of the gospel which is faithful to the way of Jesus and
the prophets. It is a response whose starting point is contemplation and
attention to the needs of the poor and outcast, not the blueprints of the
political theorist. As Gustavo Gutierrez has put it:

> Contemplation and commitment combine to form what may be called
> the phase of *silence* before God. . . . Silence is a condition for any

loving encounter with God in prayer and commitment. . . . Theology is talk that is constantly enriched by silence. In our dealings with the poor we encounter the Lord (see Matthew 25. 31–46), but this encounter in turn makes our solidarity with the poor more radical and more authentic. Contemplation and commitment within history are fundamental dimensions of Christian practice . . . The mystery reveals itself through prayer and solidarity with the poor. I call Christian life the 'first act'; only then can this life inspire a process of reflection, which is the 'second act'. (Gustavo Gutierrez, *The Truth Shall Make You Free*, p. 3).

To me that sounds like a theology which is rooted in the heart of the gospel of a person to whom injustice and violence were done, for it seeks to take seriously the reality of the suffering of the majority of our world.

8 Reading the Gospels Seriously

Enoch Powell

My contribution to this series of lectures may well appear to be none at all. If so, that is a symptom of my own difficulty in grasping the nature of the Church into which I was born and to which I belong. It is a difficulty that assails me grievously when invited to reflect upon the relation between the doctrine and liturgy of the Church and the political affairs which have been my predominant concern for the last forty or fifty years.

When others refer for chapter and verse to the book of that Church I find myself confronted with an absorbing intellectual task, which challenges, while it defies, my full comprehension.

There are five books in the Christian library known as the New Testament which purport to be narratives. Four of them purport to be narratives of the acts, words and death of a central figure called Jesus. A reading from these narratives accompanies each performance of the major acts of worship of the Christian Church, upon which they furnish a kind of commentary and to which their reading has from a very early date been integral.

They can, however, also be read quite differently. They can be read in order to learn how and why they came to be written as they are, and what they have to tell us about past events in human history. We can read Caesar's *Commentaries* in that way, and we can read the gospels in that way – in a word, as objects of study.

If we read them as objects of study, we read them as we would read any other narrative works, with all our critical faculties alert and introducing no assumptions or information derived from outside. I have ventured, for the sake of the title, to describe this procedure as reading the gospels 'seriously'. It involves readiness to admit to ourselves when we are not understanding what we read, a determination not to stifle the still, small voice which says, 'But *that* is nonsense', or alternatively, 'Why should any rational human being have written *that*?' If we are surprised by what appears not to have surprised anybody before, we are not entitled to persuade ourselves that we are not surprised at all. If we arrive at conclusions contrary to our previous assumptions or otherwise unwelcome, we

shall not on that account suppress the conclusions but rather see whether
they lead to further conclusions.

Without thus reaching a conclusion as to how and why the gospels
came into existence in their written form, it must be unsound and even
dishonest to use them as a source of binding moral or political authority.
The study is frequently detailed and even microscopic; but there is no
reason to be deterred on that account, because the evidence which documents exhibit of their origin and composition is frequently of that nature.

The first observation which we cannot avoid making is that there is a
large measure of overlap or coincidence between the first three gospels
and to a lesser degree between all four. If they were written by independent witnesses or on the information of independent witnesses of the
same real events, that would be expected. What would not expected is
the degree of verbal similarity between the parallel accounts. It is a degree
of similarity which could only occur if there were either mutual copying
of one by another or copying of a common text by two or more of them.

The consequences of this observation are so far-reaching that the
student can proceed no further until he has settled what the relationship
is. If B has copied A, any differences of B from A must be due to B
having either altered what he read off his own bat or having had access
to other information. If we do not like the idea that things in B are B's
own invention, we can of course assume that B had information from
a source other than A; but it is not beyond the capacity of the human
mind to settle the question between those alternatives. Judges and juries
are doing that very thing every day. In particular, if difficulties in A's
wording explain the differences found in B, it will be probable, especially
if the alteration is awkward, that the author of B made the changes himself
and that he possessed no independent source. The oftener this happens, the
higher will be the probability, amounting eventually to certainty, that A was
B's only source. We shall then have to take this into account in assessing items in A which B omits and items which B has that are not in A.

It is high time for me to illustrate this abstract reasoning with a concrete
example. The so-called Sermon on the Mount has hardly got started when
we read in Matthew (5. 13): 'You are the salt of the earth; but if the salt is
made foolish' – that is an accurate translation of the Greek (*mōranthē*) –
'with what shall it be salted? It no longer avails for anything but to be
thrown out and trodden underfoot by men'. That sounds like gibberish,
and it *is* gibberish; but before the student enquires how the gibberish got
there, he takes a look at Luke (14. 34, 35): 'Salt is a fine thing; but if the
salt too is made foolish' – the same word, *mōranthē* – 'with what shall

it be flavoured? Neither for earth nor for dunghill is it fit: they throw it out'. Luke has done his best, but still he is in a mess. He did not dare change the word 'be made foolish', persuading himself perhaps, like modern scholars, that it could mean 'become insipid'; but he made a gallant attempt at repair, replacing the striking phrase 'you are the salt of the earth' with the lame 'salt is good', trying to help out with 'too' (if the salt too . . .'), and rewriting the rest because 'treading salt under-foot' was more than he could abide. He never asked himself where any-thing goes which is 'thrown out', if it is neither on the ground nor on the midden; yet he had to mention 'the ground' because the phrase 'salt of the earth' was haunting him. At least he avoided 'salting salt' by sub-stituting 'flavour' (*artuthēsetai* for *halisthēsetai*).

The student thereupon, perceiving that Luke did his best with Matthew, takes a peek at Mark (9. 50): 'For everyone will be salted with fire. Salt is a fine thing; but if the salt become unsalty, with what will you flavour it? Have salt among yourselves and keep peace with one another'. What has happened? Mark has taken from Luke 'salt is good' and the verb 'flavour' (*artuein*); but feeling that he needed a context, Mark hooked the saying about salt onto hellfire from another part of the Sermon (5. 29, 30) by pivoting on the verb *halisthēsetai*, 'be salted', which he illicitly treated as if it meant 'be purified'. Thus, after transcribing Luke's rewrite, he wound up with a practical applica-tion, a moral application, which presupposes a trilingual pun, *hals* Greek, *sal* Latin and *shalom* Hebrew, 'peace'. So a moral precept has vanished into thin air.

Before we start to talk about Our Lord making trilingual puns, it is incumbent to define the relationship between the same item in each of the three gospels. The connection between them is not accidental: each step in it is verbally demonstrable and visibly motivated. Above all, there is only one direction in which the changes can seriously be held to have taken place – namely, Luke from Matthew and Mark from Luke. Any alternative route, such as to start with Mark and attempt to explain the derivation of Luke from Mark or of Matthew from Luke fails to provide a logical explanation. The consequence is that the gibberish in Matthew must be treated as either the original or the nearest which we posses to the original; and serious study must address itself to the question of how that original arose.

At this stage, however, I am only concerned with the basic importance of establishing relative priority. Once established, it obliges the student to take the first gospel as the archetype and concentrate upon that, ignoring the others as derivative. As such, the first gospel presents arresting features which demand explanation. I present a specimen of one of those features.

The temptation in the wilderness is followed in Matthew at 4. 12 by these words: 'And when he heard that John was arrested, he withdrew to Galilee'. That is a monumental gaffe; for this is the first the reader ever knew or suspected about John's arrest. It cannot be brushed off as if it meant 'see below chapter 14. 2 for a full account of the arrest of John'. On the contrary, John's arrest is mentioned again below at 11. 2 as something already known to the reader.

All this confronts us with a duty, with the duty to explain why an account of John's arrest was deleted and what the implications of that are. We are not completely in the dark. The return of the Holy Family from Egypt (2. 22, 23) was followed immediately by a potted biography of John the Baptist and an account of how Jesus was baptised by him. This is introduced by the words '*in those days* arrived John the Baptist'. Now, the words 'in those days' are dead wrong: in the context, 'those days' have to be the days of Jesus' infancy, whereas in the account of his baptism he is evidently already adult. (Luke saw the problem and filled the gap with anecdotes of the childhood of Jesus.) It is curious, incidentally, that, though John is called 'the Baptist' as if notorious, the reader should be given a concise briefing about him as a fresh character.

So John has been foisted roughly onto a pre-existing text, with the purpose, presumably, of baptising Jesus whom he acknowledges as his superior.

By taking sufficient trouble it is possible to identify the place where the passage which has been deleted originally stood. That is a task which Luke, who realised what was missing and supplied it, attempted but unsuccessfully. He put John's arrest, which is narrated in stilted language betraying the writer's embarrassment, in what might be thought the natural place – after the potted biography and before the baptism of Jesus. That is not where it originally stood. In the telltale sentence which put us upon this enquiry the words 'withdrew to Galilee' obviously referred back to 3. 13, 'then arrived Jesus from Galilee at the Jordan where John was, to be baptised by him'. They provide as it were a frame to span one or more items in between, which must therefore have included not only the baptism of Jesus but the arrest of John.

One other clue is the word 'heard' ('when he *heard* that John had been arrested'). This proves that the arrest took place in Jesus' absence. Since that absence was not due to his return to Galilee, it can only relate to the temptation in the wilderness, which the deleted arrest therefore followed. It would in any case have been embarrassing for Jesus to be standing by idly while John was hauled away. It was bad enough that his only reaction to the event was to return home to Galilee. He evidently came back from the wilderness and was told by somebody – we shall presently guess by whom – 'John has been arrested'.

We are now in a position to outdo Luke and compose our own substitute for the missing passage. 'Now, while Jesus was in the desert, Herod, who was outraged (*aganactēsas*) by John's prophecies, sent soldiers, arrested him while he was baptising, and took him into custody. His disciples told Jesus on his return what had happened; and when he heard that John had been arrested he withdrew to Galilee'.

For those who enjoy coincidences, when the full account of John's arrest and execution eventually does come at chapter 14, it ends with the same words (14. 12, 13): 'His disciples went and told Jesus, and when he heard he withdrew (the same word, *anachōrein*) to a solitary place'.

Between the first appearance of the Baptist which we have just been examining and that account of his death, he puts in another appearance at 11. 2: 'And John, hearing in the prison the works of Christ, sent by his disciples and said to him, "Art thou he that is to come or are we to expect someone else?".' The words 'in the prison', like the telltale phrase we have just investigated, imply the existence of the deleted narrative of John's arrest, to which they are a clear reference. But there is something peculiar. The encounter between John and Jesus at the baptism is written to imply that John already knew the identity and divinity of Jesus. The interrogative at 11. 2 serves only the function of producing a resounding declaration from Jesus himself about the Baptist's importance.

So we have to confront the fact of the deletion of the original notice of John's arrest. The reason which it assigned for that arrest cannot have been the same as that which precedes the account of his execution; for this latter, connected as it is with Herodias and Herod's marriage affairs is designed to lead directly into the story of Salome and the decapitation. This later account of his arrest rendered the earlier notice of it superfluous if not incompatible and motivated its hasty deletion – how hasty and rough-and-ready, is proved by the fact that the open wounds left behind by its excision remained unattended to.

Thus a series of interlocking textual problems forces upon the serious student of the gospel an important insight. The appearances of John the Baptist are insertions in a pre-existing document concerned with Jesus, and the job was done roughly and without subsequent editorial polishing.

The operation was motivated by a desire to distinguish Jesus sharply from John while nevertheless attributing to John an important status. In particular, the insertion of the story of John's decapitation was itself an afterthought.

We may, if we wish, speculate upon the circumstances in which the possessors of a Jesus-gospel sought, or needed, to conciliate the possessors of a John-narrative. For that speculation, however, evidence of a different kind would be required. It would include the startling affirmation by Herod, which is used as the occasion for narrating John's execution in prison, that Jesus is none other than John 'risen from the dead' (14. 7). At all events, one of the peculiarities of Matthew, of which the other gospels would have left us unaware, is the adventitious nature of John the Baptist's appearances. We are in the presence of something which recalls the eerie sensation that overtakes the listener when, in the middle of the introduction of John's gospel, he is startled by the strange denial, uncalled for by its context, 'he [John] was not that light'. Somebody had evidently said, or at least supposed, that John *was* Jesus.

Another phenomenon which no serious student has the right to overlook in Matthew is the presence of duplication. The most blatant instance is the miraculous feeding of the multitude (Matt. 14. 15–21, duplicating 15. 30–39). That this duplication is a literary phenomenon and not due to the reporting of two actual events is capable of cogent demonstration.

The miraculous feeding of a large multitude with bread which Jesus breaks, blesses and distributes is not with sincerity to be separated from the eucharist. The action is, in plain terms, an allegory of the eucharist. The allegory moreover culminates in a declaration not merely of the total numbers fed there and then but of the quantity of receptacles necessary to contain the left-overs which were collected afterwards.

Recognition of the incident as allegorical has far-reaching implications – in particular for the explanation of the duplicates. There may, in theory, be two distinct, though virtually identical, events which can be reported and recorded as such. There cannot however be actual repetition of an allegorical event. An allegory is not history. It not only does not require repetition for its validity: it is inconsistent with repetition. So the two narratives, which are verbally akin, though with notable and therefore presumably intentional verbal differences, could have originated only from one another; and since there was no point in repetition in the same book, they must have stood originally in different books.

The line of reasoning which has compelled us to reach that conclusion cannot terminate there. It obliges us to envisage two further conclusions. First, the derivative book was designed to counter or supersede its exemplar; and secondly, the exemplar and the book derived from it were subsequently combined together, without regard for stylistic considerations, to form the basis of what we know as the Matthew gospel. That gospel, then, is the product and the evidence of some sort of concordat or compromise. The difference between the two feedings turned upon the difference between, respectively, twelve and seven boxes or baskets containing the left-overs. That difference must have been allegorically significant; but since it is inconceivable that the two books differed only at this particular place, it would be rational to seek less crassly obvious duplicates elsewhere in Matthew, and, having identified them, to elicit the reasons, theological, liturgical or otherwise, for the divergences.

To do so would carry me far beyond the self-imposed limits of this lecture. Its purpose will have been achieved if it has suggested that serious study of the gospels confronts the student with problems which he cannot burke and still retain a good conscience, if 'He that made us, with such large discourse looking before and after, gave us not that capability of godlike reason to fust in us unused'. They are problems which arise inescapably from the detail of the text. Yet, if confronted, they lead into regions apparently far remote from textual and literary criticism.

The gospels go back to an archetype represented by Matthew. That archetype was the product of fusion between an earlier book and a derivative intended to displace it; but into that archetype has subsequently and hastily been introduced the figure of John the Baptist as the inferior but the forerunner of Jesus. About the Church which possessed such a book this much at least can be asserted, that it identified Jesus as the Son of God and that it celebrated the Eucharist.

We have found ourselves the reluctant spectators of an eventful process from which emerged the earliest form in which we possess that Church's book, a form which later reflection and elaboration have conspired to obscure. It hides the secret of an episode in the religious life of the ancient world played out perhaps against the backdrop of violent events.

The methods which have yielded these preliminary results are still unexhausted. It is not impossible that they may yet illuminate the profoundly obscure connection between that episode and those events. What is not foreseeable is that they will provide an authoritative source of moral and political guidance to those whose form of worship is older even than the Church's book itself.

9 How Can We Discharge our Obligations to the Poor?

Digby C. Anderson

A social policy which is informed by Christian understanding is about both needs and obligations. The poor, homeless, orphans, and the sick have needs. So, in a slightly different sense, do members of an advanced society have needs of education. Their fellow men and women have obligations to help the less fortunate satisfy such needs. Much time and many pages have been spent recently on detailing the needs. Much less has been said about the obligations. This chapter tries to correct the balance by asking, 'How, today, should I discharge my obligations to those less fortunate than myself?'

There is one tradition within the church which does not appear to think the question that difficult, or rather it appears to treat it as a secondary matter. According to this, possession of wealth is the major problem and how to dispose of it is dictated by the need to get rid of something which carries temptations and potential distractions from the spiritual life.

St Paul does not say this but he says enough, for example in the first letter to Timothy (ch. 6) to make this one legitimate development of doctrine.

> 'We have brought nothing into the world and we can take nothing out of it: but as long as we have food and clothing, let us be content with that. People who long to be rich are a prey to temptation; they get trapped into all sorts of foolish and dangerous ambitions which eventually plunge them into ruin and destruction. "The love of money is the root of all evils" and there are some who, pursuing it, have wandered from the faith, and so given their souls any number of fatal wounds.'

True, this is a message for wealth-seekers rather than the wealthy but he goes on, 'Warn those who are rich in this world's goods not to look down on other people; and not to set their hopes on money, which is untrustworthy'. There is little considered thought here for the poor: the interest is in the dangers of the would-be-rich to themselves. Riches, or at least the acquisition of riches present a danger to the rich rather than exploit a denial of the poor. This may be taken to legitimate extremes. Thus St Athanasius, in his *Life of St Antony* (ch. 2–4), tells how St Antony, the outstanding father of all monks, heard the gospel in church about Christ telling the young man to sell all he possessed and give to the poor and follow him. Athanasius explains that the saint 'immediately' went out and gave away to the villagers 'some three hundred very fertile and pleasant acres – so they would not be an *encumbrance* to him'. He then sold the rest of his possessions, gave his sister a small sum and the rest to the poor. On returning to church, he heard the gospel about not being anxious for the morrow, 'could not wait any longer but went out' and gave away the small sum he had kept for his sister whom he sent to a convent. He then went off nearby to live the ascetic life.

Certainly the unburdening was done very effectively in so far as that was the object but as a model of effectively helping the poor it is not very explicit. Antony seems to have been in a tremendous hurry: did he get the best price for his goods? Did he know which villagers needed his acres most and who would best use them, what dissensions the allocation of the acres might cause? Does it matter?

Another tradition, citing Pascal's dictum making tough thinking the cornerstone of morality, suggests it does. The first requirement of morality, including charitable donations, is to think hard and maximise the need relieved. Stewardship matters as much in giving goods away as in keeping them in trust. The possession of riches is a station to which some men are called which carries with it exacting, mentally as well as financially exacting, charitable obligations. This tradition has no doubt that it matters a lot if foreign aid is generously but naively or thoughtlessly given and ends up in the hands of corrupt Third World rulers rather than in the mouths of the starving. It matters if government handouts reduce the barriers to single parenthood and attract more people into need, if benefits create unemployment or poverty traps, if welfare creates and institutionalises a culture of poverty.

According to this tradition, the obligation to give involves an obligation to think about the efficacy of the particular form of giving. It would answer the question of 'How to discharge obligations to the poor' with 'thoughtfully' as well as 'generously'. But the question posed above contained another complication. It asked how to help the poor *now*.

My view, and that of many welfare analysts across the political spectrum, is that while the obligation is eternal and unchanging, the means are not. We would hold, and I put it first at its weakest, that discharging welfare obligations or, if you will, answering the question, is more difficult now than it was 20 years ago. Uncontroversial? Well, let us beef it up a little: answers which were good enough 20 years ago are not good enough now. Shall we drive the lesson home? Intelligent people who are giving the same answer today as 20 years ago are not only giving an inadequate answer but failing in their moral duty to *think* about the obligation and discharge it as *efficiently* as possible.

Now you see how apparently innocuous questions can have far from innocuous implications. For the charge that I and others have repeatedly made is that the Church has been recycling old, tired and failed solutions to problems which are now seen not only to have changed but to have become more difficult to understand and respond to. It is partly a question of mood. The recent history of events – the practical snags social policy has run into in the past years – those poverty traps, welfare dependency, the perverse effects of well-intended legislation – and the exposure of the full, ghastly and murderous chaos of the regimes which tried out socialist solutions most 'thoroughly' in eastern Europe coupled with the recent history of ideas, the intellectual problems of social policy – have made analysts cautious, sceptical and hesitant. Who of them now, for example, would want to be held responsible for a policy to cure crime? Who has any confidence that there are clear, simple reforms of income support and social security which would solve problems without creating others?

Today *how*, exactly *how* to discharge the obligation is the key issue. Technical embarrassment and modesty in the face of social problems are no longer the preserve of naturally cautious conservatives but epidemic among socialists and free marketeers as well. Reticence reigns universal in social policy – except in the Church.

There, it is still heroes and villains stuff, rallying calls to action, manipulative and inaccurate divisions of the entire population into comfortable and suffering, charges of government neglect with the comfy implication that there is indeed some obvious policy being neglected, a naive belief in the efficacy of public spending, a downright dishonest portrayal of the tax-welfare system as somehow automatically helping the poor and therefore in need of more or less unqualified boosting and behind it all a quasi-marxist credulity in the explanation of complex social problems by 'structural' factors. This persistent and wilful travesty is suffused with a sloppy and sentimental rhetoric of care and compassion which is no substitute for a precise morality.

That, at any rate, is Church poverty-speak at its worst. But even better versions show the same tendencies. Consider the Urban Fund appeal: much concern was expressed originally about how to raise the money; whether, indeed, it would be raised. Hardly any was expressed about how to spend it. I mean that spending it was not seen as a problem. Were there not legions of projects whose realisation only awaited funding? No problem in how to spend. But I suggest, and I could muster a large number of policy analysts to support me, that spending it as *efficiently* as possible is indeed the problem, that spending it so that perverse and unintended effects do not accompany and even exceed the desired results is indeed a problem, that redistributing income optimally – for that is what the Urban Fund is about – is a daunting task requiring not breezy confidence but humility.

Let us summarize how the problem is emerging. Recent years have seen real world events and intellectual developments which mean that state welfare can no longer be assumed to be effective welfare. Those of different political persuasions can argue over the extent and character of its successes and failures. That balance sheet does not concern us. What is not controversial is that it can and does go seriously wrong to the extent that it cannot be taken for granted. The obligation to welfare involves then an obligation to *think* about whether in this or that case state welfare will indeed deliver the goods. Those who refuse to think, who assert today that the welfare state does indeed deliver welfare merely on the grounds that it was once intended that it should do so are not discharging their moral obligation. Clergymen and bishops who confuse the way the tax systems works with the way they would like it to work are failing both the poor and those who seek guidance on their obligations from them.

Let me try and very briefly summarize a checklist of the shortcomings to which state welfare is liable, that is, a list of the things a thoughtful and moral philanthropist will want to satisfy himself do not obtain before he endorses the State as the means of discharging his obligation. This list is a version of one which appeared in the *Social Policy Review*, 1988–90, edited by Nick Manning and Clare Ungerson (Longman).

The object of many social policies is the redistribution of wealth directly, or in the case of education indirectly, by redistributing 'life-chances' and social mobility. It is widely alleged that the welfare state has failed substantially to shift wealth from rich to poor or to increase social mobility. The state education system was repeatedly reformed under Labour governments on just such grounds. Higher education, in particular, is notorious for the way it takes taxes from poor families to subsidize the degrees – and later enhanced earning ability – of children from middle-class homes. Nationalised health services fail to give lower-income earners the extra health care they disproportionately need. Though social security may redistribute from rich to poor, the net effect of it combined with tax relief is much less benign.

Not only is welfare said not to get to those in need but a significant part of this perverse welfare is funded by those in need. A consistent theme of criticism, especially in the early eighties, was that those below official poverty levels are paying standard-rate tax to subsidise benefits to middle-income groups. Taxation, traditionally said to be the proper way of funding benefits to the poor, is itself causing poverty.

It is also charged that much welfare provision does not transfer income at all, returning benefits or services in similar proportions to the amount taxpayers have paid – minus freight charges in both directions. Frequently cited is the refusal to amalgamate social security and inland revenue calculations, a duplication of benefit neither to taxpayers nor claimants but providing employment for civil servants.

State welfare involves a salaried 'welfariat' which has its own interests. Both socialist and non-socialist analysts have claimed that it is liable to 'producer capture' by the welfariat who run it for their purposes rather than those of its clients and tax paying funders – social workers who 'controlled' clients and 'dominant' doctors. The insight of the school known as 'the economics of bureaucracy' has been the way that officials are driven by their own motivations, an echo of the revision of the Weber thesis known as the 'development of intermediate goals'. In brief, there is no reason to assume that because an organization is set up to help pupils, the unemployed or the insane that helping those people will be the actual everyday goals of persons working in the organisation. Nor are those employed in public service inherently more altruistic than those employed in private.

Also from work inspired by public choice as well as a more general market economics came the contrast between political and economic preference. Producers of goods sold in the market know what their customers want by how they respond to goods offered at a range of prices. Daily the shopkeeper is instructed by his sales on which goods the customer values most and which more than others – all at very precise intervals. Welfare goods, e.g. health products, are not sold in the market and their producers get no such detailed information about their customers' preferences.

Two problems emerge. First, in the absence of prices and known preferences, the producers decide how much of what goods are to be provided. Rationing is done by the diktat of the producer – the doctors, social services director, Minister of Health decide who is to be helped and who not, who is to live and die – rather than by price. Second, the information they do receive about customer preferences is very crude. Customers vote but their votes do not record their views of different departments, let alone of specific services and they are unweighted –

they give not the slightest hint of how *much* the goods are valued. They simply endorse political parties with packages of policies.

This failure of politically registered preference compared to economically registered preference not only adds to producer dominance but means that even a producer keen to serve the customer is deprived of the information he needs about what people want and how much they want it.

This ignorance of customer preferences is but one to which state welfare is liable. Social policy needs knowledge of the extent and character of the problems it is to tackle, tried and tested solutions to those problems, methods of delivering solutions on a mass scale and methods to evaluate its policies. It is highly questionable whether it has such knowledge. In the absence of market information it must rely on social scientific research which, despite its many other fine qualities, is less than totally reliable as practical policy knowledge.

The fact that the social world is orderly and known by its members in an intuitive, practical and untheoretical way does not necessarily mean that this knowledge is available to a central body or in a form necessary to plan intervention. So often social interventions are justified on their desirability: but the key question is 'does the government have the knowledge to solve the problem?' Do we know how to avoid poverty and unemployment traps without creating other problems, how to target benefits, how to reduce the numbers of future lone parents without stigmatizing current ones, how to stop landlords exploiting tenants without drying up the rental market, how to curb drug abuse?

This ignorance is not only a handicap but a potential danger. Welfare is not only done by governments but is the effect of millions of individuals caring for each other, parents for their children, neighbour for neighbour. This spontaneous, uncoordinated, dispersed welfare is much bigger than the government sector. Thus one risk is that government policies, whether successful or not in themselves, might disrupt, disable or subvert informal welfare or the institutions such as the family which deliver it so prolifically.

Welfare is often discussed in terms of equality and a safety net but the theme of standardisation is also a frequent goal, the theme that it should not matter who someone is or where they live, they ought to have standard services. The discovery that schools are not standard and that their results vary to the tune of 500 per cent within local education authority from the best to the worst, or the more recent Department of Health assessment that, using a series of measures such as cost and length of stay and waiting list time, some hospitals appear 10 times as efficient than others are especially concerning. Supporters of state welfare claim that markets fail to deliver standard care – they are haphazard. So apparently is the welfare state.

There are numerous other criticisms of state welfare. It is pointed out that we have now seen it in expansion and contraction and it does not appear to manage either particularly rationally: i.e. it cannot handle change. Again, it is argued that the values it promotes are inimical to enterprise and self-reliance and thus endanger true welfare.

It is difficult to establish just how much damage these criticisms do to the welfare state: some say they are fatal, others that these are but accidents and drawbacks. All that concerns the present discussion is this: these are serious enough to make it unreasonable to *assume* that paying one's taxes is discharging one's welfare obligations. Our individual is then to a greater and lesser extent brought back to deciding for himself how to discharge his obligations which may well include cheerfully funding state welfare. That is what I mean about it being more difficult. One cannot take the efficiency of the welfare state for granted. Put more positively, he is brought back to questions not so much of state welfare but of welfare itself.

What is his next step? Well he could do worse than think about precisely to whom he is obliged. Saint Antony gave away all his wealth to his fellow-villagers. Why not the men of the next village who might have been worse off? Perhaps he had read the advice of the rabbis cited by our own Chief Rabbi designate, Jonathan Sacks (in *L'Eylah*, September 1988) that "the poor of your town take precedence over the poor of the next town".

Sacks, in the passage quoted, is discussing whether claims to compassion are universalistic or particular, whether we have greater obligations to some rather than others. Most of the criticisms of state welfare, such as those above, have been about whether it is efficient and effective in fulfilling its aims. while one or two of those aims, for example equalizing people, do not enjoy everyone's support and some would rather see welfare as a safety net than a general right, nevertheless the broad principle that each of us ought to be helping the less fortunate is widely accepted. In this formulation, although this is rarely spelt out, 'those less fortunate' means those in our society or nation and sometimes those in the world.

And yet this surely is open to question, exception and limitation. How much do we owe to all? Do we not owe more to family than neighbour and more to neighbour than those far away, more to those with whom we come in contact and less to those we do not come across, more to our own countrymen and less to foreigners. To say otherwise would go against the grain of gut morality and make a nonsense of social institutions and order. What family, what community, what nation could survive such a levelling and anomic imperative? Social order is based on discrete and particular loyalties and duties.

The very term 'community' and its use, some would say over-use, by churchmen, if it means nothing else – which is often the case – means that we owe more to some than others, more to those in than those outside the community. It is to this extent in tension with 'citizenship', that other vogueish platitude, which stresses what we owe to all under the same government. Are rights and obligations universal, national, local or familial?

The idea that we owe more to some than others is deeply embedded in both Judaism and Christianity. The rabbis, writes Rabbi Jonathan Sacks, were explicit 'What does it profit a person if he saves the whole world and neglects those closest to him. The poor of your family take precedence over the poor of another family.' He goes on, 'there were few more telling symptoms of the universalism implicit in Western culture than the failure of the world to be moved by Israel's rescue of Ethiopian Jewry. "Jews rescue their own" was the cynical reaction. To which the Jewish response is instinctively: "if we are *not* the kind of people who will rescue our own, are we the kind of people who will ultimately rescue anyone?"'

Christian socialists are much given to citing the parable of the Good Samaritan to justify state welfare. It is certainly true that the welfare urged in the parable is one which transcends racial and religious barriers. Yet it is far from undiluted universalism. The parable teaches not so much obligation to all men as obligation to *any* man in need. It has nothing to say about guaranteeing the welfare of all. And the any man to whom welfare obligations are owed is not some sought-after, still less theoretically defined, opportunity but the man whom we come across, whom we find near to us by the side of the road. Proximity and localness are the themes, and rather particularistic ones at that. (The Good Samaritan is discussed by me in the *Journal of Social Policy*, 19, 4, 553–5, 1990.)

There are, of course, universalistic themes in the gospels. We have obligations to each man because he is made in the image and after the likeness of God. The Incarnation hallows fleshly humanity and we are bidden to find Christ in the hungry and the imprisoned. Christian love is for each man. At the same time, it is quite clear that Christ had a special love for his Mother: as the hymn has it. 'Shall we not love thee Mother dear, whom Jesus loved so well?'

Christianity (and note I acknowledge and emphasize these) of course has universalistic or perhaps we should say similitudinal themes but it also has its particularism. And it is a fairly clear particularism. We are called to a complex web of differentiated loving: not only does Christ have a special love for the Virgin Mary, he is shown loving St John, the 'beloved disciple' in a special way. His long address in the upper room on the night before his death is a meticulous legacy in which different gifts and obligations are allotted particularly as between the apostles and other, a meticulousness on which the Apostolic churches are founded. His grief that first Holy Week was sharpened by grief for his own people, the Jews, because he loved them particularly.

This is a difficult balance to hold. Cardinal Newman writes of God's providence, stressing its discriminating universality in the most moving way, 'Thou art careful and tender to each of the beings that Thou hast created as if it were the only one in the world . . . Thou lovest everyone in this mortal life, and pursuest every one by itself, with all the fulness of Thy attributes, as if Thou wast waiting on it and ministering to it for its own sake' (John Henry Newman, *Meditations and Devotions*, p. 92, Burns and Oates, 1964).

But it does not follow that man can love with the same incredible blend of universality and particularity. Newman himself writes elsewhere, 'How absurd it is when writers talk magnificently about loving the whole human race . . . The best preparation for loving the world at large . . . is to cultivate an intimate friendship and affection towards those immediately about us.' Again, 'There have been men before now, who have supposed Christian love was so diffusive as not to admit of concentration on individuals; so that we ought to love all men equally . . . Many neglect the charities of private life, while busy in the schemes of an expansive benevolence.' And he pours scorn on the attempt to love abstractions such as Humanity (All from *Parochial Sermons*, ii, 52–5). Indeed several biographers have remarked on the role of *friendship* in his life. It is something which also come across in the gospels in the life of Christ himself.

A further particularism, for which justification is sought not only in St John himself but in what Cullman calls the Johannine Circle and Brown the community of the beloved disciple, is the notion that members of the community of the Church have obligations to each other which take some sort of precedence over their obligations to non-members. Another is the the co-obligations of monastic communities.

These particularisms are not meant to be exclusive. The Catholic principle of subsidiarity stresses the discharge of obligations by those nearest others in need, near geographically and in terms of relationships. Look first to family, then to neighbourhood, then to State. But this is meant to radiate out so that everyone discharging their own discrete obligations results in all or most being cared for.

But however effective the radiation, it can in no way be represented as like a state standardized or universalistic and comprehensive welfare system. It has none of the planned directness of state welfare nor the supposed guarantees that none will fall through the net. Moreover, of all levels of human aggregation, family, neighbourhood, State, international community, it is the State which receives the least endorsement from the gospels. Apart from honouring the king and obeying laws, St Paul has little to say about the State. The Good Samaritan undercuts the state level in his concern for the needy man nearest you, and over-rules it in his dismissal of racial and religious boundaries to obligation. If any further evidence were needed that one cannot *assume* one's charitable obligations are automatically fulfilled and exhausted by paying even high taxes – and even in Sweden – it is the sheer high demand of Christian particularistic-universalistic welfare. For loving all is easy compared to the fine and discriminate fulfilment of particular relationships to which Christians are called combined with the universalism which finds Christ in each and commands that men love as he did.

And there is another complication to think about. Welfare is not the only Christian obligation. Another is to follow God's laws and to be the sort of people He wants us to be. Christianity has a morality as well as a charity. More than that, it was thought, until recently, that this morality was indeed a form of charity, that teaching or enforcing certain standards was an act of kindness to, especially, the young. This is the nub, *the* modern welfare problem, for many of the newer welfare problems do not fall from the sky on their victims – as do the problems and needs of old age – but result at least in part from their victims' own behaviour. Single parenthood which follows illegitimacy or divorce, drug addiction which follows experimentation, health problems resulting from alcohol misuse, poverty which springs from unemployment and idleness, are all problems in which the victim is more than passive – though not necessarily guilty. Thus comes the Churches' problem, how to help those in need without devaluing standards and without lowering the barriers and encouraging others into positions of need in the future. Ways are suggested. Conditionality is one, whereby benefits are dependent on a change of behaviour. Proximity is another; the emphasis that helpers must be close to those in need to know their precise problem. But whatever the solution, indiscriminate giving is not it, that is giving which treats poverty as simply monetary and shows no interest in the individual circumstances of the poor. Thus, there is reason to be wary of the language of rights in poverty, the notion that by virtue of being poor to a certain degree, the person has a right to such and such a benefit at the same level as another of the same degree, without enquiry as to circumstances or imposition of conditions.

These three groups of problems which the conscientious philanthropist has to think through, the criticisms which have been made of the welfare state, the puzzles of particularity and universalism and the conflict between upholding standards and helping the needy in behaviour-related poverty must make any thinking person cautious before assuming that his payment of taxes to the current state system is discharging his obligations. But there is worse. The nineteenth-century sociologist Herbert Spencer, who had little time for state welfare, pointed out that welfare could come from other sources (the first of which he had reservations about as well); voluntary welfare, that is organizations voluntarily set up to help those in need, and what we might call informal welfare, that which occurs when a mother looks after her child, a young couple their elderly parents, a neighbour his disabled neighbour.

Look through the criticisms of state welfare and you will find that a large number also potentially apply to voluntary welfare. It too can become remote. Its workers can substitute their own goals for those of the organization. They are deprived of market information about their clients' needs and may have no sure knowledge of how to deal with certain problems, such as drugs or child abuse. Some of them find it difficult to contract or expand 'rationally' and they have no easy answer to the conflict between maintaining standards and providing help. True, such of these and other problems which are mitigated by good local information about those in need may be reduced in those organizations with strong local ties. True, too, their lack of comprehensiveness can mean that their help does not encourage further dependents because it is not a right known comprehensively to be available.

Yet many voluntary bodies are increasingly close to the welfare state. Some supposedly voluntary bodies receive regular state funds. Some of their employees are trained with and share a common welfare culture with those who work in state welfare departments. And the voluntary societies are, like the state bodies, increasingly unionised with the unions demanding that the societies divert more of their funds to those who work in them. Yet other apparently welfare societies do not so much do any welfare work as confine themselves to urging the Government to spend more on this or that. They are simply lobbies for more taxation, more state welfare. And all this is without looking at the problems of international agencies dealing with underdeveloped countries chronicled recently in Graham Hancock's *Lords of Poverty*.

Once again, it must be clear that this does not mean that no voluntary organisation does its work well. What it means is that one cannot *assume* that any of them does so.

Spencer's third category is the most attractive. Not only is there a gut moral feeling that we ought to be helping especially those immediately around us – family, neighbourhood, those at work — but there are sound welfare-efficiency reasons for doing so. Here, at last, donor knows recipient, his needs, any behavioural complications, history, and can give effectively and quietly. But a modern society does not always encourage such ties of family and neighbourhood as make this possible. They are not eroded as much as some have argued but they are far from being an adequate or universally reliable basis for the satisfaction of need and the discharge of responsibility.

There has been talk during the eighties of a crisis in state welfare. I happen to think that crisis indeed exists. But the point of this chapter has been to argue that it is not just a state welfare crisis but a welfare crisis. That the three main channels for helping the needy are cracked, twisted or blocked to the extent that they cannot be assumed to be effective. That is bad news for the needy. It is also bad news for the would-be charitable. There are large numbers of people who have money of their own or more to the point, are likely to inherit large sums, people who are not ungenerously disposed. If they are St Antonys, they have no problem, but what if they take their obligation to help the poor intellectually seriously, what – and I emphasize the words – *exactly* and *today*, should they do?

10 Unto Caesar: The Political Relevance of Christianity

David McLellan

Over the last decade the political importance of religion has become more evident than many would have predicted in the 1950s and 1960s. In North America the arrival of Jimmy Carter in the presidency provided evangelical Christians with a sense of legitimate political mission. Christian duty and responsible citizenship were once again united and the 1980s saw the rise of the New Christian Right which, although it seems to have peaked around 1986 or '87, achieved a dismayingly high level of political influence; in South America we see the spread of a radical Catholicism drawing on Marxist social analysis and known as liberation theology; and in eastern Europe the role of the Churches in fostering the movements of opposition is widely known. Even in the comparatively secular enclave of the United Kingdom, it is not only the reaction of some Muslims to *The Satanic Verses* that has brought the question of the relationship of religion to public authority to the fore: there has recently been a surprisingly sharp attack on the values underlying the British government's education policies by the leader of England's Roman Catholics, Cardinal Hume, and a fresh assault on the same government's neglect of inner cities which has placed fresh strains on relations between Downing Street and the Anglican establishment. The original report *Faith in the City*, published in 1985, was described by Cabinet ministers as 'pure Marxist theology' – an evidence of their depth of disagreement, if also of their ignorance, both of theology and of Marxism.

Against this background, my aim is to offer a general discussion of the relevance to politics of religion – and particularly the Christian religion as this is the only one likely to be familiar to most of my readers, and certainly to myself. In so doing I do not intend to provide answers to these very vexed questions, though it will no doubt be clear where my own preferences lie. My aim is the more modest one of trying to sketch out a framework which will perhaps enable us all to reflect more fruitfully on these matters. To this end, I want briefly to review the classical political theoretical tradition where it deals with these questions; then, via a glance at the text 'Render Unto Caesar', to discuss the view that Christianity is irrelevant to politics either because it just is, being

110

other-worldly, or because, in as far as it is this worldly, it is simply a reflection of political arrangements and therefore has no relevance in the sense of being an independent variable. Thirdly, I will suggest, more substantially, that religion is not solely a dependent variable but has some substantial influence sometimes on the society in which we live – and therefore is a fitting subject of interest for all, whether they be believers or not. Fourthly, I shall have a few negative words to say about the view that, although religion may well in fact *be* influential, this is inappropriate in a liberal democracy. Finally, after some rather caustic remarks on Margaret Thatcher's version of Christianity, I shall conclude by sketching out what does seem to me to be a suitable dialectic between politics and religion. These remarks are intended to set the scene for the 'case studies' which follow and are designed to elaborate on these general themes.

The founding father of all thought on this subject in the Christian West is undoubtedly Augustine. However much early Christians such as Tertullian may have been indifferent and even hostile to the State, the adoption under Constantine of Christianity as the official religion of the Empire posed the question of the appropriate relationship of Church and State that has been with us ever since. Augustine's answer, in the famous nineteenth chapter of *The City of God* is in terms of two cities, the heavenly and the earthly, which are in fact two societies, that of the saved and of the reprobate. This makes Augustine's answer capable of many interpretations for the two cities are by no means co-extensive respectively with Church and State.[1]

Mainstream Christianity has seen the State as, in some sense, divinely ordained. In Augustine, the State is a result of the Fall and a bulwark against Sin; in Aquinas, more optimistically, it is seen as part of the natural created order; even in Luther with his very strong separation of the Two Kingdoms, spiritual and secular, the authority of the State derived ultimately from God. The classical political theorists do not depart from this tradition. Machiavelli, in his *Discourses*, saw religion as a strong political cement and declared that 'the princes of a republic or a kingdom must maintain the foundations of the religion they have; and having done this, it will be an easy thing for them to keep their republic religious, and in consequence, good and unified.'[2] We may or may not accept the argument of Howard Warrender who reduces all obligation in Hobbes to an ultimate obligation to obey God,[3] but there is undoubtedly a strong analogy in Hobbes's thought between the role of the sovereign and that of God. And he can refer to Leviathan itself as a 'mortal God'.[4] In Locke, 'all legitimate authority everywhere and always exercised by one human being over another is an authority conferred upon that person ultimately by God'[5] and his whole theory of rights depends on his view of the universe as divinely created.[6] Although Rousseau might at first sight seem to put forward a very radical form of Christianity, in practice he is ultra-conservative and his proposals for a civil religion are designed simply to uphold the sanctity of the social contract and the laws. Indeed it almost seems to be a professional tendency of political theorists to subordinate religion to politics – or attempt to exclude it altogether: otherwise it just become too troublesome.

This latter view that religion is, and should be, separate from politics only came into prominence in post-Enlightenment societies.[7] It has constantly been supported by reference to the text referred to in the title of the present work: 'Render therefore unto Caesar the things that are Caesar's and unto God the things that are God's'. The rules of God, in other words, are one thing – those of politics and the State are another: separate spheres. But it should be noted that the Christian tradition has, from Tertullian onwards, offered a slightly different interpretation. On the several occasions in which the wily Pharisees try to entrap him, Jesus usually responds by undermining the presuppositions of the question. The word render – *apodote* in the Greek original – is better translated 'give back': return to the source from which it came. Just as the penny should be given back to Caesar since it bears his image, so to God should be given back what bears God's image – that is humankind made in God's image and likeness. The 'and' in 'and unto God the things that are God's' here has the sense of 'but': give pennies to Caesar, but yourself to God, an overriding obligation which might be thought to include and indeed subordinate the political.[8]

But this merely reveals the text to be ambiguous – and complex questions are, of course, rarely resolved by appeals to texts, slogans or even principles. So I now wish to examine in a broader context the two positions outlined above. Take first the view that Christianity is, or should be, irrelevant to politics. Examples from the history of the United States might be adduced in support of this position. The early Pentecostalists of the nineteenth century were left-leaning with a rhetoric not far from that of the International Workers of the World, but after 1920 they became political conservatives anti-evolution, anti-communist and anti-Al Smith – without any change in their religious doctrines.[9] In the antebellum South fundamentalist protestants did not want their biblically-inspired moral views to be embodied in legislation – but they have held very different views on that question in the 1980s.[10] Or consider Mary Fulbrook's discussion in her book *Pietism and Politics* of the very different contributions made by the Puritan and Pietist movements to the success or failure of absolutist rule in England, in Wurttemberg and in Prussia where the same religious ideas and aspirations led to quite different political attitudes and alliances depending, so she claims, on the structural context.[11] In more recent times, both Jesse Jackson and Jerry Falwell lay claim to the support of the evangelical Protestant tradition.

But, even in these examples, it is important to note that Christianity is not strictly speaking irrelevant to politics: the most that is being claimed is that, in these instances, it is not the specific content of the religious beliefs that is efficacious: religion plays a role, sometimes crucial, but the fact that it can do so is not due to the particular doctrines but to the general context in which these beliefs are deployed. This context is inescapably socio-political. The demand that bishops adopt the same attitude to economists that the Pope should have adopted to Galileo – respect for the professional expert – is based on a fallacious assimilation of social to natural science. Indeed, the view that Christianity, as an otherworldly religion concerned with personal redemption, etc., is devoid of political content seems to be just wishful thinking. It is a view propounded by that pre-eminently wishful thinker, J-J. Rousseau who in his *Social Contract* declared: 'Christianity as a religion is entirely spiritual, occupied solely with heavenly things; the country of the Christian is not of this world. It is true that he does his duty; but he does so with profound indifference to the good or ill success of his efforts'.[12] Various forms of contemporary existentialist theology have continued this attitude and concerned themselves almost exclusively with the authenticity of existence in inter-personal relationships. It is also a view more recently expressed by Edward Norman in his controversial Reith Lectures of 1979. But even this approach does, of course, itself have inescapable political implications, of a conservative nature. It is no accident, as the Marxists like to say, that Norman was Dean of Peterhouse. It is also worthwhile pointing out that the very survival of the Christian religion depends on its collective memory as embodied in its language, ritual, artefacts, etc. The preservation of these depends, at least in part, on political arrangements and the retention of the social power to ensure their preservation.[13]

If, then, Christianity is condemned to have some political relevance, what is its nature? (I leave aside here the extreme views of such thinkers as Voegelin, Dawson, or even Berdyaev, who see all political systems of which they disapprove as, at bottom, a species of religious heresy.[14]) One, but not the only, positive version of the connection between Christianity and politics is as a reflection and legitimation of the structure of political power. And this is often allied to a thesis about the social deter-

David McLellan

mination of religious beliefs of which traditional, orthodox Marxism is the starkest expression. This tends to restrict religion's relevance to a minimum by dismissing religion as an instrument of class rule, an ideological bulwark of the dominant class. This view contains a convert ontology, both in the simplistic equation of the origin of a belief with its truth value and its assumption that religious assertions must always be a cloak for something else, obviously so in the case of conservative religion but equally so in the case of radical religious movements – Anabaptists, Cargo Cults – which must be cloaks for political demands. The traditional Marxist metaphor from heavy engineering – base and superstructure – tends to put religion on the tip-top of the superstructure and thus at the farthest remove from 'reality'. Functional accounts of religion following Durkheim, though capable of greater subtlety, go even further in denying autonomy to the religious sphere and indeed deny to the notion of religion any substantive content. The definition of religion here as society's ideal self-description is too wide for my purposes. Yet even if we give the notion of religion a more substantive content, we can see that there is much truth in Durkheim's approach. In the rather less static version of it proposed by Robert Bellah, there are striking parallels between the religious dynamism and the economic dynamism of the United States. Images of God *do* often mirror existing dispositions of political authority. For Nietzsche, the levelling-down mediocrity of modern democracy was just a secularization of the slave mentality of Christianity that he so despised. A lot of liberal protestant theology in the United States has been devoted to dismantling ideas of an autarchic and monarchical God in favour of a more federal democratic conception.[15] In this regard the pragmatic ideas of James and Dewey were taken up by Whitehead to reveal a picture of God not as the un-moved mover, the great Before who created the universe *ex nihilo* – but as someone who continually brings order out of chaos (*e pluribus unum*!) in some sort of dynamic interdependence with the universe. Whitehead rightly said that in post-Constantinian Christendom 'the Church gave unto God the attributes which belonged exclusively to Caesar';[16] what he did not realise was that the many process philosophers and theologians of his own day were doing exactly the same.

Or, to move across the Atlantic, consider the images of God which have accompanied the rise of the welfare state in Britain over the last century and more. Here both liberal progressive theology and political theory coincide in depicting both God and the State in terms of bureaucratic benevolence. As the contemporary State has increasingly taken over and co-ordinated the functions of patronage and of charity that previously rested in disparate private hands, so the monolithic God of Protestantism has come to usurp all the various tasks, protective and entrepreneurial, that had previously lain in the hands of angels and saints. As one writer has recently put it 'today God is thought of by many as the celestial grandmother indulgently handing out benefits and performing more satisfactorily the role which an under-financed welfare state tried vainly to fulfill'.[17]

Yet the opposite is also true: however often religion may indeed be no more than the flowers on the chain, the halo above the valley of tears, it can also be the sign of the oppressed creature, the heart of a heartless world – and in a more effective sense than Marx intended. Conceptions of God can serve as a conscious focus of opposition to prevailing ideas and arrangements – images of an alternative society. We need only think of the emergence of black theologies, particularly in the United States, which refuse to accept the white man's God. Or, more radically, feminist theologies which find ludicrous the idea of a God who, as in the traditional story of the fall of Lucifer, could mind that an angel should try to fly higher than Him – the word 'Him' being, of course, used here advisedly. To take a narrower and more specific example: it has been plausibly argued that immediately prior to the 1935 general election in New Zealand 'the religious variable exerted considerable independent influence on social change, by legitimating the agents of change – the Labour Party – and by suggesting specific innovations that the Labour Party might adopt in order to bring about a specifically Christian solution to the problem . . . it was by producing religious symbols to interpret the situation that the religious institutions exerted an independent influence on the changes that occurred'.[18] Here the role of religion, and particularly theology, is that of producing symbols which legitimize otherwise unpopular beliefs, and thus enable them to gain increasing acceptance. Although religious belief rarely determines outcomes, the affinity between religion and socio-political attitudes pointed out by writers such as de Tocqueville and Weber does afford religion an influence that is often under-estimated.

That this should be possible involves conceding that religious belief can act as a partially independent variable in the social and political process. Both the Marxist and the Durkheimian traditions find it difficult to concede this. The anarchist tradition, however, has taken religion much more seriously: recall the lengthy polemics of Proudhon and Bakunin against the idea of God as necessarily authoritarian – or of Nietzsche against the idea of God as necessarily weak. The point here is that theology can be both a dependent *and* an independent variable:

theology, and religious belief in general, are socially constructed realities – but that means that they are both socially constructed *and* social realities. The most important doctrinal controversy in the early history of the Christian Church was the Arian heresy which revolved around the question of whether Jesus was of like substance to the Father or of one substance – *Homoousios* or *Homoiousios* – the difference of a single letter. That an argument about a single letter could be so prolonged, so bitter, and so threatening to the very foundations of the Roman Empire may seem to some like a species of collective dementia.[19] Not so. The Arians by denying godhead to Jesus left God the Father as an isolated Emperor in heaven best represented by a solitary tyrant on earth: a strong form of Trinitarian doctrine, by contrast, offers space for a more pluralist kind of politics. To take an example from nearer home: different interpretations of Protestantism produce different conclusions about the value of involvement in politics: whereas the Baptist 'free will' tradition still makes the average church member in the United States reluctant to see religious doctrines carried through into politics, the Calvinist tradition which is far stronger in the North of Ireland than in the United States, leads to a tendency for the saints to impose their version of righteousness on the unregenerate.[20]

But it might be argued, although religious belief does in fact affect people's political attitudes, this is inappropriate in a liberal democracy and we should strive for its elimination. In a liberal democratic society, in other words, the grounds of decision should have an interpersonal validity that extends to virtually all members of society. Decisions should be based on shared premises or types of reasoning that are accessible to everyone. Although the theories of liberal democracy advanced by John Rawls and Bruce Ackerman do not explicitly mention religion, its exclusion is implied. In Rawls, for example, the 'veil of ignorance' behind which people are to choose the principles of justice which will govern their society includes ignorance of their particular conceptions of the good. More recently Rawls has written: 'In public questions ways of reasoning and rules of evidence for reaching true general beliefs that help settle whether institutions are just should be of a kind everyone can recognize',[21] which seems to exclude religion. But it seems to me simply untrue that important political questions can be resolved on the basis of value premises that are shared by all or even on shared approaches to factual knowledge. To see the force of this, one has only to reflect on the arguments surrounding such issues as the possession of nuclear weapons, our attitude to the environment, or to abortion. It is unfortunately the case that in very many important issues rational grounds for assessing what is true are highly inconclusive; and when that happens people are likely to rely on some sort of deep and intuitive feelings; and this often involves a religious perspective. To say this is not to undermine any vital premise of liberal democracy: it is to recognize the fact that citizens in a liberal democracy rely generally on moral judgements to arrive at decisions, and that moral judgements are frequently informed by religious views. It is also to recognise that liberal democracy is less anaemic than many of its proponents would have us believe. And it is also compatible with the view that, as far as open public discussion is concerned, it is mistaken for the ordinary citizen to advocate a position by direct reference to his or her religious values – general human welfare being the appropriate point of reference. Where you get your values from is up to you: the terms in which you advocate them to your fellow-citizens is more circumscribed. If you are a church leader where your job is to express the views of your specifically *religious* community, the case is, of course, different. But, by contrast, the tendency of *political* leaders to refer to the Deity should be resisted – both because of the tendency to homogenize religion and the usually arrogant presupposition of the coincidence of their country's progress with the purposes of God.

An arresting example of what can happen if the above warning is not heeded is provided by Margaret Thatcher. She is quoted as saying that, if the Churches took sides on practical issues, 'this can only weaken the influence and independence of the church, whose members ideally should help the thinking of all political parties'. Which seems to amount to saying that the Churches can be very influential so long as they do not actually try to influence anything. This reminds me of the non-apocryphal churchwarden writing a letter to the bishops of the type of person they hoped would be appointed to the vacant post of parish priest: 'Our experience and reports we have heard of politically active clergy in this part of the county compel us to believe that such a ministry would be neither beneficial nor fruitful'.[22] Underlying this utterance is the assumption that being a supporter of the Conservative Party is not to be politically active.

According to Margaret Thatcher, in her speech to the General Assembly of the Scottish Church in 1988, the distinctive marks of Christianity stem not from the social but the spiritual side of our lives – note the sharp dichotomy. They consist in the triad: the belief in the doctrine of Free Will; in the divinely-created sovereignty of individual conscience; and in the Crucifixion as the supreme and exemplary act of choice. They all, you will note, boil down to the individual's right to choose – Christ's choosing to die on the Cross is merely the forerunner of those who have chosen to buy their own council house, occupy pay-beds in National

Health Service hospitals, or send their children to private schools.[23] And in outlining her views about the relevance of Christianity to public policy – the things, as she puts it, that are Caesar's – she gives a breezy summary of both the Old and the New Testaments and finds therein another three key elements: a view of the universe, a proper attitude to work, and principles to shape social and economic life.

Now a 'view of the universe' sounds as though it were merely an attractive and desirable amenity, like a view of the sea. But with 'the proper attitude to work' we get more down to it. Here, together with the principles that shape social and economic life Mrs Thatcher might, vainly, have hoped to establish common ground with her audience who were, after all, grounded in the Calvinist tradition. For, to quote Raban,

> like Calvin himself, Mrs Thatcher will have no truck with mediating institutions. On this, the record of her government is both logical and exemplary, with its attacks on the Church, the BBC, and the universities, on powerful agencies of local government like the Greater London Council, and even (especially over South African sanctions) on the monarchy. She is passionately 'anti-statist' – yet every institution which has traditionally stood between the individual and central government has been either abolished or has come under heavy fire from her administration. If the Kingdom of Man is a shadowy reflection of the Kingdom of God, then Margaret Thatcher is a good Calvinist; for it is emerging as a fundamental principle of 'Thatcherism' that individuals shall stand as nakedly before their Government as they do before their Maker.[24]

The point is that here there is too close a relationship between religion and politics. Mrs Thatcher's narrow, thin, simple, petit-bourgeois (in the worse sense) attitude to economics and politics has colonized the religious sphere – and impoverished it almost beyond belief. Its American equivalent is the evangelical Christian who is quoted as saying: ' "Give and you'll be given unto" is the fundamental practical principle of the Christian life, and when there's no private property you can't give it because you don't own it . . . Socialism is inherently hostile to Christianity and Capitalism is simply the essential mode of human life that corresponds to religious truth'.[25] *All* this kind of politicization of religion – like that of art and literature – is to be resisted. But – and this is my argument – it cannot be resisted by relegating religion to a separate sphere. It is just not possible: the two are substantially connected. A jejune politics (and Thatcher has a *very* jejune approach to politics) will yield a jejune religion. But the reverse is also true: a bigoted or superficial or not sufficiently materialist religion will equally have à deleterious effect on politics. From this point of view the dictum of Marx needs to be reversed and the criticism of politics needs to issue in the criticism of theology; and those inside Churches must make sure that their own organizations and practices at least come up to the level of the standards that they are advocating for society at large.

If Tertullian's interpretation of my text is right and men and women are made in God's image, then they should enjoy the maximum of effective freedom. But, in Britain and elsewhere, this freedom is currently being taken away from local government, from the universities, from trade unions as power become ever more centralized in Westminster, Whitehall and the City of London – a process which the Churches are being asked to legitimize by preaching traditional moral values to shore up an ever stronger State. Under these circumstances it would be a mistake for those who oppose such policies and values to fail to leave some space for religion in their approach to society and politics. For religions are difficult, in the long run, to co-opt and to have their essential values corrupted by power. It is, I believe, significant that at the end of 1989 the demonstrations in Dresden and Leipzig rested on a base in the Lutheran Church while the guerrillas of El Salvador depend crucially on their Church's base communities. Nearer home, the intellectuals and cosmopolitan élites may be steeped in post-modernism, but it is religion, charismatic and evangelical, that stalks the inner cities. It may be, as MacIntyre has forcefully argued, that so many of our modern aporias spring from the fact that our moral sense has been uprooted from any shared tradition of belief and story about our past.[26] But religion in some shape or form has been a deep and enduring aspect of human activity – and there is every reason to think that this will continue to be so for at least the near future. Benign neglect or outright rejection by the left will mean that the immense power of religion can be captured by the ideologies of the right. Consider here the recent role of the so-called 'moral majority' in America and the way in which, almost by default, a whole string of repressive social measures appear to many there to have behind them the weight of the whole Judaeo-Christian tradition.

My argument is that, however you personally may read that tradition (and I think it is oppositional rather than establishment), it is possible and legitimate and advisable to use it to afford a critical perspective on the political problems of the present time. The most apparently abstract metaphysical beliefs are, at the same time, severely practical. Thus the notorious polemic of William James towards the end of his *Varieties of Religious Experience* is misplaced. James pours scorn on 'the metaphysical attributes of God' and claims that 'from the point of view of practical religion, the metaphysical monster which they offer to our worship is an absolutely worthless invention of the scholarly mind.'[27] James's view is, of course, a function of his own – equally metaphysical – brand of Cartesian individualism. All politics involves metaphysical choice,[28] and we are all as inescapably metaphysical as we are political.

NOTES

1. See further: P. Brown, 'Political Society', in *Augustine: A Collection of Critical Essays*, ed. R. Markus, Garden City: Doubleday, 1972.
2. *The Discourses of Nicolo Machiavelli*, ed. L. Walker (London: Routledge & Kegan Paul 1975) vol. I, p. 244. See also S. Da Grazia, *Machiavelli in Hell* (Princeton: Princeton University Press, pp. 119ff., 376ff.)
3. Cf. H. Warrender, *The Political Philosophy of Hobbes* (Oxford, Clarendon Press, 1957).
4. T. Hobbes, *Leviathan* (Oxford: Blackwell, 1946) p. 57.
5. J. Locke, *Two Treatises on Civil Government* (New York: Mentor Books, XXXX) p. 181.
6. See further: J. Dunn, *Interpreting Political Responsibility* (Cambridge, Cambridge University Press, 1990) ch. 2.
7. See J. Crimmins, ed., *Religion, Secularization and Political Thought. From Locke to Mill*, (London: Routledge & Kegan Paul, 1989).
8. For a summary of recent exegetical research here, see: F. Bruce, 'Render Unto Caesar', in E. Bammel and C. Moule, *Jesus and the Politics of His Day*, (Cambridge, Cambridge University Press, 1984).
9. R. Moore, *Religious Outsiders and the Making of Americans* (New York: Oxford University Press, 1986) pp. 144ff.
10. Ibid., pp. 156ff.
11. Cf. M. Fulbrook, *Piety and Politics* (Cambridge: Cambridge University Press, 1983) pp. 174ff.
12. J-J. Rousseau, *The Social Contract and Discourses* (New York:Dutton, 1973) p. 274.
13. Cf. N. Lash, *Theology on the Way to Emmaeus* (London: Darton, Longman & Todd, 1986) p. 70.
14. See J. Shklar, *After Utopia: The Decline of Political Faith* (Princeton: Princeton University Press), pp. 170ff.
15. Cf. D. Nicholls, *Deity and Domination* (London: Routledge & Kegan Paul, 1989) ch. 5.
16. A. N. Whitehead, *Process and Reality* (New York: Scribner, 1978) p. 342.
17. D. Nicholls, op. cit., p. 30.
18. H. Wieman, 'Some Blind Spots Removed', *The Christian Century*, vol. 39, 1939, p. 61.

19. See, for example, the ironical commentary of Gibbon in *Decline and Fall of the Roman Empire*, ed. Burg, London, 1896, vol. 2, pp. 344ff.
20. For a stout defence of the claim that the conflict in Northern Ireland is, among other things, a deeply *religious* conflict, see P. Badham, *The Contribution of Religion to the Conflict in Northern Ireland* (Canterbury: Centre for the Study of Religion and Society, 1988).
21. J. Rawls, 'Justice as Fairness: Political Not Metaphysical', *Philosophy and Public Affairs*, vol. 14, 1985, p. 539.
22. Quoted in P. Hinchliffe, *Holiness and Politics* (London: Darton, Longman & Todd, 1981) p. 6.
23. I am merely summarising here the splendidly amusing and incisive critique of the Thatcher speech by Jonathan Raban in his *God, Man and Mrs. Thatcher* (London: Chatto & Windus, 1988).
24. J. Raban, op. cit., pp. 34f.
25. George Gilder, quoted in R. Wuthnow, The Restructuring of American Religion (Princeton: Princeton University Press), p. 248.
26. See A. MacIntyre, *Whose Justice? Which Rationality?* (London: Duckworth, 1988).
27. W. James, *Varieties of Religious Experience* (New York: Longmans, 1902) p. 447.
28. Cf. J. Maritain, *Le Philosophe dans le cité* (Mulhouse: Vie Nouvelle, 1960) pp. 9ff.

Further Reading

Anderson, Digby (ed.), *The Kindness that Kills*, London: SPCK, 1984.
Anderson, Digby, *Secondary Poverty Rediscovered*, London: SAU, 1991.
Badham, Paul (ed.), *Religion, State and Society in Modern Britain*, London: Edwin Mellen, 1984.
Benn, Tony, *Arguments for Socialism*, London: Jonathan Cape, 1979.
Benn, Tony, *Arguments for Democracy*, London: Jonathan Cape, 1981.
Benn, Tony, *Fighting Back*, London: Hutchinson, 1988.
Benn, Tony, *Speeches*, Nottingham: Spokesman Books, 1974.
Benn, Tony (ed.), *Writings on the Wall*, London: Faber & Faber, 1984.
Berryman, P., *Liberation Theology*, London: Tauris, 1987.
Bradley, Ian, *God is Green*, London: Darton, Longman & Todd, 1990.
Butler, B. C., *Originality of St. Matthew*, Cambridge: Cambridge University Press, 1951.
Chafuen, Alejanoro, *Christians in Freedom*, New York: Ignatius, 1986.
Cohn-Sherbok, Dan, *On Earth as it is in Heaven: Jews, Christians and Liberation Theology*, Maryknoll Orbis, 1987.
Cohn, Haim, *Human Rights in Jewish Law*, New York: Ktav, 1984.
Corner, M. and C. Rowland, *Liberating Exegesis*, London: SPCK, 1990.
Ellis, Marc, *Toward a Jewish Theology of Liberation*, London: SCM Press, 1987.
Forrester, Duncan, *Theology and Politics*, Oxford: Blackwell, 1988.
Gill, Robin, *Beyond Decline: A Challenge to the Churches*, Oxford: Mowbray, 1988.
Gutierrez, G., *A Theology of Liberation*, 2nd edition, London: SCM, 1989.
Habgood, John, *Church and Nation in a Secular Age*, London: Darton, Longman & Todd, 1983.
Heschal, Abraham, *The Prophets*, London: JPS, 1962.
Jacobs, Louis, *A Jewish Theology*, London: Darton, Longman & Todd, 1973.
Kee, Alastair, *Constantine or Christ?*, London: SCM Press, 1982.
Kessler, Edward, *An English Jew*, London: Vallentine Mitchell, 1989.
Locke, John, *Letter Concerning Toleration*, The Hague: Nijhoff, 1963.
Lohfink, Gerhard, *Jesus and Community*, London: SPCK, 1985.
Montefiore, Hugh, *Christianity and Politics*, London: Macmillan, 1990.
Macintyre, Alastair, *After Virtue*, London: Duckworth, 1981.
Mesters, *Defenseless Flower*, London: C.I.I.R., 1990.
Our Common Inheritance, London: HMSO, 1985.
Pearce, D. et al., *Blueprint for a Green Economy*, London: Earthscan Publications, 1989.
Preston, Ronald, *Church and Society in the Late Twentieth Century: The Economic and Political Task*, London: SCM, 1983.
Sacks, Jonathan, *The Persistence of Faith*, London: Weidenfeld & Nicolson, 1991.
Saunders, E. P., *Jesus and Judaism*.
Seldon, Arthur, *Capitalism*, Oxford: Blackwell, 1990.
Theissen, Gerd, *The First Followers of Jesus*, London: SCM, 1978.
The Gaia Atlas of Planet Management, N. Myers (ed.), London: Pan Books, 1985.

The State of the Word 1990, Washington DC: Worldwatch Institute, 1991.
Vincent, John J., *Radical Jesus*, Basingstoke: Marshall Pickering, 1986.
Vincent, John J., *Britain in the 90s*, London: Methodist Publishing House, 1989.
Vincent, John J., *Discipleship in the 90s*, London: Methodist Publishing House, 1991.
Ward, Keith, *The Rule of Love*, London: Darton, Longman & Todd, 1990.
Witvliet, T., *A Place in the Sun*, London: SCM Press.
Writings on the Wall, ed. Tony Benn, London: Faber & Faber, 1984.

Index

Abortion, 7
Ackerman, Bruce, 116
Aquinas, Thomas, 111
Athanasius, St, 98
Augustine of Hippo, 111

Base Ecclesial Communities, 47, 74, 76ff., 119
Bakunin, Michael, 115
Bellah, Robert, 11, 114
Benjamin, Walter, 85
Berdyaev, Nicholas, 113
Boff, Clodovis, 74
Boff, Leonardo, 82, 88
Boniface, Pope, 6
Brazil, 75ff.
Buber, Martin, 29
Bush, George, 35

Calvinism, 118
Camara, Helder, 86
Carter, Jimmy, 110
Catholic Church, 8f., 30, 61, 85, 110
Christendom, 2, 17, 19, 22, 24, 26f., 114
Church of England, 5ff., 11, 14ff., 20, 26, 31, 61
Clarke, Ramsay, 32
Cohn, Haim, 67
Communism, 21
Cox, Percy, 34
Creation, 52

Daube, David, 69
Dawson, Christopher, 113
Dewey, John, 114
Diabetic, 13
Divorce, 7
Dulles, Foster, 34
Durkheim, Emile, 114

Education, 12, 22f.
Elliott, Charles, 81

Ellis, Marc, 72
Enlightenment, 9
Environment, 3, 22, 24, 52ff.
Establishment, of the Church, 2, 5ff., 15f.
Euthanasia, 7

Falwell, Jerry, 113
Fuentes, Carlos, 87, 89
Fulbrook, Mary, 112

Gandhi, Mahatma, 37
Global warming, 58ff.
God, 1, 3, 6, 8, 75
Grenada, 35
Guttierez, Gustavo, 80f., 89ff.

Habgood, John, 62
Hancock, Graham, 109
Harris, 'Bomber', 34
Harrod, Dominic, 29
Henry VIII, 5, 30
Hobbes, Thomas, 111
Horsley, Samuel, 72
Hume, Basil, 110
Hussein, Saddam, 34ff.

Imperialism, 34
Incarnation, 51

Jackson, Jesse, 113
James, William, 114, 119f.
John Paul I, 7
Judaism, 64ff., 70f., 87, 104

Kairos, 42ff.
Kingdom of God, 42, 50, 118
Kuwait, 34ff.

Labour Party, 30f.
Law, Natural, 9, 18, 38, 51f.
Liberalism, 2, 9f., 18f., 22f., 81f.
Liberation, 3, 48, 74ff., 110

Lloyd, Selwyn, 34
Locke, John, 6, 68, 111f.
Luther, Martin, 111

Machiavelli, Niccolo, 111
MacIntyre, Alasdair, 119
Maimonides, 69
Mao Tse-tung, 29
Markets, 53
Marxism, 24, 87, 110, 114f.
Marx, Karl, 30, 115, 119
Materialism, 24
Maxwell-Fyfe, David, 71
Mendelssohn, Moses, 70
Mesters, Carlos, 83
Mill, John Stuart, 19
Miranda, Jose, 74
Montagu, Lily, 64
Montefiore, Claude, 64

Newman, John Henry, 106
Niebuhr, Reinhold, 70
Nietzsche, Friedrich, 114f.
Norman, Edward, 113
Novak, Michael, 89
Nuclear energy, 55
Nuclear weapons, 24

Old Testament, 1, 31
Owen, David, 29

Panama, 35
Pascal, Blaise, 99
Pluralism, 14, 22, 27
Poland, 1
Pope Innocent, 33, 111
Population control, 57f.
Presbyterian Church, 20
Privatisation, 20, 25

Prophetic tradition, 65ff.
Proudhon, Pierre-Joseph, 115

Raban, Jonathan, 118
Ramsey, Michael, 61
Rawls, John, 116
Reagan, Ronald, 35
Reformation, 7f., 30
Religion, 1, 14, 21, 30
Rights, human, 18, 23, 71, 73
Rousseau, Jean-Jacques, 112f.
Runcie, Robert, 65

Sacks, Jonathan, 104f.
Secularism, 10
Secularization, 27
Smith, Al, 112
Socialism, 31, 118
Spencer, Herbert, 108
Stalin, Joseph, 29
State, 2, 5ff., 8, 16, 19ff., 23f., 111, 114f.

Tertullian, 111, 119
Thatcher, Margaret, 60, 111, 117f.
Thirty Nine Articles, 11
Tocqueville, Alexis de, 115
Trujillo, Lopez, 74

United States, 25, 68, 114

Vatican Council, Second, 7
Voegelin, Eric, 113

War, 2, 30ff., 35
Warrender, Howard, 111
Weber, Max, 115
Wilson, Harold, 29
Winter, Derek, 81
World Council of Churches, 61